Forestry Commission
Handbook 11

# Creating and managing WOODLANDS AROUND TOWNS

Simon J. Hodge

LONDON : HMSO

ISBN 0 11 710328 4

FDC 270:62:91:(410)

British Library Cataloguing in Publication Data
A CIP catalogue record for this book is available from the
British Library

**KEYWORDS:** Amenity, Conservation, Design,
Establishment, Landscape, Management,
Urban forestry.

**Published by HMSO and available from:**

**HMSO Publications Centre**
(Mail, fax and telephone orders only)
PO Box 276, London, SW8 5DT
Telephone orders 0171-873 9090
General enquiries 0171-873 0011
(queuing system in operation for both numbers)
Fax orders 0171-873 8200

**HMSO Bookshops**
49 High Holborn, London, WC1V 6HB
(counter service only)
0171-873 0011  Fax 0171-831 1326
68-69 Bull Street, Birmingham, B4 6AD
0121-236 9696  Fax 0121-236 9699
33 Wine Street, Bristol, BS1 2BQ
0117 9264306  Fax 0117 9294515
9-21 Princess Street, Manchester, M60 8AS
0161-834 7201  Fax 0161-833 0634
16 Arthur Street, Belfast, BT1 4GD
01232 238451  Fax 01232 235401
71 Lothian Road, Edinburgh, EH3 9AZ
0131-228 4181  Fax 0131-229 2734
The HMSO Oriel Bookshop
The Friary, Cardiff CF1 4AA
01222 395548  Fax 01222 384347

**HMSO's Accredited Agents**
(see Yellow Pages)

*and through good booksellers*

## Acknowledgements

The production of this Handbook would not have been possible without the contributions of:
- Derek Patch, Arboriculture Advisory and Information Service (refereeing)
- George Gate, Forestry Commission Research Division (photography and graphics)
- Pat Hunter Blair and colleagues in the DANI Forest Service (help, information and Plates 10.1, 10.2, 10.3, 10.4 and 10.5, and Figure 10.1)
- Gareth Price, Forestry Authority England (design of Freckland Wood, comments on text and Figures 9.1 and 9.2)
- Simon Bell, Forestry Commission Forestry Practice Division (Figures 10.2, 10.3, 10.4 and 10.5)
- Dee Stamp and Community Land and Workspace Ltd (community involvement)
- John Williams, Forestry Commission Research Division (line drawings)
- Environmental Management Consultants (Figures 8.1 and 8.2)
- Elaine Dick, Forestry Commission Forestry Practice Division (artwork in Figure 9.3)
- Dave Rogers, Forestry Commission Research Division (Plates 6.3a and 6.3b)
- Clive Carter, Forestry Commission Research Division (Plate 7.5)

The development of the ideas and approach of the Handbook have been much influenced by working with:
- colleagues at Alice Holt, in particular Ian Collier, Derek Patch, Gary Kerr, Paul Tabbush, David Williamson and Ralph Harmer
- the Thames Chase Community Forest team (also for Figure 3.2)
- Nerys Jones and the Black Country Urban Forestry Unit (who also provided Plates 1.3 and 3.1, and commented on the text)
- Martin Glynn, Nottinghamshire County Council (who also provided the contract schedule and gave comments on Chapter 9)
- Steve Potter, Staffordshire County Council

I am grateful to the following for their valuable comments on the text:
- Clive Davis, Cleveland Community Forest
- Sheila McCabe, Department of the Environment
- George Barker, English Nature
- Gina Rowe, British Trust for Conservation Volunteers
- Vincent Goodstadt, Strathclyde Regional Council
- Paul Tabbush, Gary Kerr, Ralph Harmer, Peter Gosling, Marcus Sangster, Brian Hibberd, Andy Moffat, Richard Ferris-Kaan, Julian Evans, Graham Gill and Sally York (all Forestry Commission)

**Front cover**
Multi-purpose woodlands in the urban environment of the West Midlands. (*40956*)

# Contents

# Foreword

We tend to think of woodlands as part of the countryside but, over recent years, there has been a growing awareness of the contribution they can make to the urban environment and the quality of life of city dwellers. Urban woodlands bring the countryside and its wildlife right into the city. Managed with the involvement of local people they can encourage a sense of community ownership and responsibility and develop an appreciation of woodland and the natural environment. People of all ages working together can help to manage the woodland for present and future generations.

This vision lies at the heart of the many community and urban forestry initiatives now in place, and has attracted people from all walks of life. These people are faced with the task of realising their vision, often on heavily used and degraded sites, and many in private ownership. Success requires the skills of the forester, community worker, landscape architect, ecologist, planner and negotiator all rolled into one.

I commend this practical Handbook to all those engaged in the task. In a lively and accessible format it describes how to plan, create and manage multi-purpose urban woodlands, based on the experience gained by the Forestry Commission's Research Division in creating demonstration woodlands in association with Local Authorities and Community Forest Teams.

The Rt. Hon. Ian Lang,
*Secretary of State for Scotland*

# Introduction

Great Britain has a population of 57.4 million of which 46 million live in towns and cities and do not have immediate access to the countryside. The primary role of urban forestry is to provide woodlands and trees which improve the quality of daily life for these people.

Urban forestry is becoming increasingly recognised as a discipline in its own right but those involved come from many backgrounds and disciplines, ranging from planning through landscape design and horticulture to forestry. These backgrounds often result in an approach that is focused on certain aspects of the process of woodland creation at the expense of others. This Handbook presents practical information on the process of urban woodland planning, establishment and management. It is designed to help practitioners to achieve results where it really matters – on the ground.

The definition of urban woodland used in this Handbook is *groups of trees in and around towns that are extensively managed to provide a naturalistic vegetation structure.* This can be achieved on areas from less than 0.1 hectare to hundreds of hectares. The establishment and management of individual urban trees is not covered in this Handbook as it is a distinct discipline with its own problems and techniques.

# Introduction

La Grande-Bretagne a une population de 57.4 millions, de laquelle 46 millions habitent dans les villes et les cités, et ainsi n'ont pas d'accès immédiat à la campagne. Le rôle primaire de la foresterie urbaine est pourvoir des bois et des arbres qui améliorent la qualité de la vie quotidienne pour ces gens.

On reconnaît de plus en plus la foresterie urbaine comme une discipline de plein droit, mais ses praticiens ont des antécédents divers et viennent des disciplines différentes telles que la planification, l'architecture paysagère, l'horticulture et la foresterie. Souvent ces antécédents en résultent que la mise au point se concentre sur certains aspects de la formation des bois au prix des autres. Ce Manuel présente des informations pratiques sur le processus de la planification, l'établissement et l'aménagement des bois urbains. Il a pour but aider les praticiens à parvenir à ses fins où il importe vraiment, c'est-à-dire sur le terrain.

La définition de bois urbain utilisée dans ce Manuel est *des groupes des arbres dans et autour des villes qui s'aménagent extensivement pour fournir une structure naturaliste végétale.* On peut réaliser ce but sur des superficies de moins que 0.1 hectare jusqu'à des centaines d'hectares. Ce Manuel ne traite pas de l'établissement et de l'aménagement des arbres individuels urbains, parce que c'est une discipline distincte avec ses propres problèmes et techniques.

# Einleitung

# Introducción

Großbritannien hat eine Bevölkerung von 57,4 Mio. von der 46 Mio. in Städten leben und keinen unmittelbaren Zugang zum Land haben. Die Hauptrolle der städtischen Forstwirtschaft ist es, Wälder und Bäume zur Verfügung zu stellen, um die Qualität des Alltagslebens dieser Menschen zu verbessern.

Städtische Forstwirtschaft wird zunehmend als eine eigenständige Disziplin angesehen, aber die Leute die sich damit befassen kommen von vielen Berufsfeldern und Disziplinen, welche von Planung über Landschaftsgestaltung und Gartenbau bis zur Forstwirtschaft reichen. Demzufolge wird sich im Verlauf der Waldschaffung oft auf gewisse Aspekte auf Kosten anderer konzentriert. Dieses Handbuch gibt praktische Information über den Verlauf der städtischen Forstplanung, Etablierung und Pflege. Es will dem Fachmann helfen, Resultate zu erlangen, dort wo es wirklich wichtig ist, nämlich vor Ort.

Städtische Forste werden in diesem Handbuch als Baumgruppen in und um Städte herum definiert, die umfangreich verwaltet werden, um eine natürliche Pflanzenstruktur zu ergeben. Dies kann auf Flächen von weniger als 0,1 Hektar bis zu Hunderten von Hektaren erreicht werden. Die Etablierung und Pflege von individuellen Stadtbäumen wird in diesem Handbuch nicht behandelt, da dies eine andere Disziplin mit ihren eigenen Problemen und Methoden ist.

Gran Bretaña tiene una población de 57.4 millones, de los cuales 46 millones habitan en ciudades y pueblos, y así no tienen aceso inmediato al campo. El papel primario de la dasonomía urbana es proveer bosques y árboles que mejoran la calidad da la vida diaria para esta gente.

Cada vez más se reconoce la dasonomía urbana como una disciplina por derecho propio, pero sus prácticos tienen antecedentes diversos y vienen de varias disciplinas – planificación, arquitectura de paisaje, horticultura y ciencia forestal. Muchas veces estes antecedentes resultan en un enfoque que concentra en algunos aspectos del proceso de la formación de bosques a expensas de otros. Este Manual presenta información práctica sobre el processo de la planificación, el establecimiento y el manejo de bosques urbanos. Tiene la intención de ayudar los prácticos de alcanzar buenos resultos donde es más importante, es decir en el campo.

La definición de bosque urbano que se usa en este Manual es: 'grupos de árboles dentro y en torno de pueblos que se manejan extensivamente para proveer una estructura naturalística de vegetación'. Este puede alcanzarse en áreas de menos que 0.1 ha hasta los cientos de hectareas. No trata este Manual el establecimiento y el manejo de árboles individuos urbanos, porque eso es una disciplina distinta con sus propios problemas y técnicas.

Plate 1.1 Urban woodlands provide opportunities for
peace and quiet, and contact with nature.

# 1 Opting for woodland

## The benefits of trees in the urban environment

Most readers who want to learn more about urban woodlands will already be convinced of the value, and committed to the provision, of trees but it is worth re-stating the benefits that trees can offer in order:

- to be clear about the case for more tree planting; and
- to make the most of trees on any given site.

Some of the most important benefits of trees are difficult to quantify.

- **Contact with nature and the seasons.** In this increasingly man-made and man-modified world, urban trees and woodlands can bring the natural environment into the town. Contact with nature is recognised to be important for keeping our urban existence in the context of the 'wider creation' and for keeping us in touch with the passage of time and the changing of the seasons. Most have experienced the positive feelings associated with seeing buds break and new leaves emerge, or the anticipation of the coming winter heralded by leaf fall.

- **The value of peace and tranquillity.** A study of an American urban forest found that perceived benefits relating to resting and escaping were especially important to users. The opportunity to relax and passively appreciate aesthetic settings appears to be a major source of the value which people place on urban parks and woodlands.

- **Spiritual and emotional renewal.** A study conducted in Sweden showed that wooded rural scenes were more effective than treeless urban scenes in sustaining people's interest and that rural scenes tended to result in lower levels of sadness and fear. Urban woodlands can promote feelings of well-being and provide a conducive setting for 'recharging the batteries'.

- **Relief from stress and improved recovery from illness.** The renowned landscape architect Frederick Law Olmstead recognised over 100 years ago the stresses of urban life and argued that views of nature are effective in helping recovery from such stresses. This has been scientifically demonstrated in American research which showed that hospital patients recovering from surgery had shorter post-operative stays and

Plate 1.2   Trees can create enclosure and a more intimate scale for urban living.

required fewer pain killing drugs when their outlook was of a small stand of trees rather than the wall of a building.

- **Improving the attractiveness of urban environments and the quality of everyday urban life.** Once people have met their basic life needs, the importance to them of environmental quality increases. A survey in the USA asked people to rate overall satisfaction with their community. Parks were the third most important issue. Research has shown that the more natural the

Plate 1.3   An absence of trees impoverishes the urban environment. (*41023*)

landscaping of streets and other urban areas, the more positively the people in the survey reacted to them.

- **Raising senses of pride of place and self worth.** Improving the quality of a neighbourhood and increasing local distinctiveness can promote pride of place and reduce antisocial behaviour. In recognition of this view, police in some American inner-city areas such as Harlem and the Bronx have become involved in community tree planting schemes. Community tree planting is also a tool for encouraging people to recognise their own worth and to learn the importance of community cooperation. For example, the RAISE (Raising Ambition Increases Self Esteem) project in Baltimore, USA has the goal of developing in participants an understanding and appreciation of nature whilst fostering a work ethic through community tree planting programmes.

Trees improve human well-being in many ways.

- **Landscape enhancement.** Trees can break up the visual monotony of uninteresting areas and reduce the perceived scale of urban development to a more intimate level. The variety of colours, textures and forms, and seasonal variations in appearance can be used to increase the beauty and diversity of the urban landscape.

- **Complementing urban architecture.** Carefully designed planting schemes or retained woodland can complement and improve the built environment by manipulating perceived scale, separating distinct architecture from its surroundings and softening the visual impact of hard development.

- **Screening.** Whilst trees cannot hide eyesores as effectively as total barriers, their natural form breaks up the harsh angularity of built structures and reduces their impact in the landscape. Trees can also screen out the surrounding area creating privacy, separation and enclosure.

- **Noise reduction.** Trees and shrubs, particularly evergreens, can be effective in absorbing noise if densely planted in belts at least six metres wide with the foliage and branches to ground level. Some researchers have contended that the ability of trees to offer an optical and psychological barrier to the source of offensive sound is just as important as their actual noise reducing capability.

- **Dust traps.** Trees are good atmospheric scrubbers and can filter out as much as 75% of particulate pollution, such as dust and soot. Species like hawthorn, which have a rounded, open canopy that allows particles easy access into the crown, are most effective. In addition, by slowing wind speeds, trees can increase the deposition of dust in their vicinity. This may be an important function of roadside planting.

- **Summer shade.** Trees cast summer shade, and cool urban areas by using energy to evaporate transpired water. With increasing concentrations of greenhouse gasses and ozone depletion, protection from direct sunlight may become increasingly important for both comfort and health.

- **Shelter.** Trees can give shelter in otherwise exposed areas and may increase the extent to which recreational activities are undertaken and enjoyed.

- **Recreation.** Urban trees and woodlands provide opportunities for recreation as well as a conducive environment for leisure and play. Surveys have shown that natural surroundings are just as important to children's games as expensive play equipment. Local woodlands are invariably a magnet for children, and areas with trees and woodland are also the best setting for many forms of adult recreation from dog walking to archery. Trees and woodlands can greatly increase the capacity of an area to absorb people and improve its ability to meet a range of recreation and amenity objectives.

- **Urban wildlife.** Urban trees and woodland can provide habitats and opportunities for wildlife to the benefit of both the flora and fauna and the people who enjoy seeing them. Because of the relatively low intensity of management in woodlands, levels of disturbance are low compared to other urban land uses and many plants and animals have the opportunity to exploit these habitats.

Trees and woodland around towns can also provide economic benefits.

- **Attracting development.** One of the main reasons for planting trees on derelict land is to cover it up and make it attractive. This important function of trees is recognised by the urban development corporations and 'City Challenge' initiatives. Improving the attractiveness of urban areas and creating a pleasant environment in which to live and work is one of the keys to drawing in commercial investment, creating jobs and improving standards of living. By injecting resources into environmental improvement at the start of this cycle, it may continue with reduced resource provision as individuals and companies seek to maintain and further enhance their own surroundings.

- **Energy conservation.** Urban trees can reduce wind speeds around buildings and so reduce heat loss from those buildings. An effective windbreak can save about 15% of the heat used in a typical home. Global warming could make the potential saving in air conditioning requirement an increasingly important consideration in this

Plate 1.4 Urban woodlands provide a wealth of opportunities for children's play.

country. There is, however, something of a dilemma as trees, particularly evergreens, shading buildings in the summer can also reduce beneficial warming of the building at other times of the year.

- **Property values.** The value people put on a well-planted environment is reflected in the price they are prepared to pay for property. In the USA trees have been shown to increase residential property values by up to 20%.

- **Wood.** Some urban woodlands and trees will have the potential to provide timber of high value, given appropriate management. Wood of lower value can still provide products like wood-chips for mulches, bark for play areas and wood for fuel.

Trees also help to maintain the quality of the global environment by locking up carbon dioxide, a gas which contributes to the greenhouse effect. As long as the wood is not burnt and does not rot down, the carbon dioxide will be kept from returning to the atmosphere. Vigorous trees lock up carbon dioxide more quickly than slow growing trees.

## Why woodlands and not just trees?

Trees provide benefits to the global environment wherever they are and however they are arranged, but the extent to which trees meet other needs depends on planting scheme design. Urban tree planting is often based on individual trees in formal designs which draws attention towards the built environment. However, in many urban situations attention needs to be drawn away from the built environment. This is best done with woodlands or groups of trees that emphasise the natural environment, through informal designs based on organic forms, and that offer the maximum opportunity for recreation, amenity and escape from the pressures of urban life.

## Urban woodland: a low-cost/high-benefit land use

Formal, high specification, urban tree-planting schemes based on large planting stock and/or planting densities up to 20 000 trees per hectare (ha) cost up to £300 000 per ha. This approach is frequently used in extensive open areas where it is inappropriate. Survival and growth are often poor and schemes soon look shabby and fail to improve the urban environment. On the other hand, urban woodland can be an extremely cost effective land use.

Urban woodland creation using forestry techniques need not be expensive. A 1.5 ha demonstration woodland was planted in 1990 by the Forestry Commission in partnership with the Black Country Urban Forestry Unit and Sandwell Metropolitan Borough Council. Woodland has been created using forestry techniques and planting stock on derelict land in the heart of the West Midlands conurbation (Plate 1.5). The total cost for site preparation and planting was £2700 per ha (1993). Maintenance costs are £240 per ha per year during the five-year establishment phase. After three growing seasons 90% of the trees were alive and 91% of live trees were growing more than 20 cm a year. The scheme is already functioning as a woodland to the benefit of local people.

The costs of urban forestry using forestry techniques also compare favourably with those of intensively managed grass sward and other soft land uses.

Plate 1.5  The Black Country urban woodland demonstration during its third growing season.

Plate 1.6  An obvious opportunity for urban woodland planting. (*38361*)

# Recognising opportunities for urban woodland

Urban trees can cause problems. Trees drop leaves, fruits, blossoms and aphid honeydew. Tree roots can damage foundations by drying shrinkable clays, make pavements uneven and block drains. Trees and branches, if blown down, can damage property and injure people. Trees can cut out light from buildings. Woodlands may be perceived as threatening places and may give cover for antisocial behaviour and crime. Careful design and species choice is essential to avoid these disadvantages.

---

**Opportunities for urban woodland creation**

When there is a change in land use, such as:

- inner city redevelopment
- redevelopment of industrial land
- reclamation of mineral workings
- restoration of landfill sites

Using vacant land:

- under-used parks and recreation grounds
- derelict urban land
- transport corridors
- urban-edge degraded farm land

---

The prospect of future development of a site should not prevent tree planting, as low-cost forestry techniques can create functioning urban woodlands in as little as three years. When development occurs, established woodland can be retained for screening and landscape improvement.

With careful planning, even small-scale opportunities can be used to improve the urban environment and to provide people with a countryside experience where they really need it: on their doorstep.

# For more information

### Publications

Anon. (1976). *Trees and forests for human settlements.* IUFRO Symposia P1.05 00, Vancouver, 11–12 June. University of Toronto Centre for Urban Forestry Studies, Toronto, Ontario M5S LA1.

Anon. (1978). *Proceedings of the national urban forestry conference.* Washington D.C. 13–16 November. Publication 80-003. State University of New York College of Environmental Science and Forestry, Syracuse, New York, 13210.

Anon. (1992). *Spon's landscape and external works price book.* E. and F. N. Spon, London.

Dewalle, D. R. and Heisler, G. M. (1988). Use of windbreaks for home energy conservation. *Agriculture, Ecosystems and Environment,* **22/23,** 243–260.

Horticultural Trades Association (1991). *Using plants to benefit the community.* 19 High St, Theale, Reading, RG7 5AH.

Ulrich, R. S. (1984). View through a window may influence recovery from surgery. *Science,* **224,** 420–421.

# 2  Issues affecting the decision to plant

This Chapter contains the following sections :

- Development plans
- Landscape protection and enhancement
- Providing a recreation network
- A long-term perspective
- Grants and advice
- Sponsorship for tree-related activities
- Urban woodlands and the law
- For more information

If you are involved in urban woodlands there are a number of issues that may affect your plans.

## Development plans

Not all urban green-space or urban fringe land should be planted with woodland, and a balance of green-space land uses is required, as well as a balance between green-space and the built environment. The development planning system provides a framework for making the most of urban space and it is important to appreciate where your woodland fits in.

At the county level, structure plans provide guidance on planning matters in accordance with regional planning guidance. Mineral plans and waste management plans are also relevant for woodland creation on reclaimed and restored sites. At the district or borough level, local plans focus regional and county policy and strategy by outlining opportunities for development and land use

Plate 2.1  A landscape of declining distinctiveness on the outskirts of Birmingham.

policies for the locality. In metropolitan boroughs these two levels of plan are combined into unitary development plans (UDPs). The purpose of these tiers of development planning is to reconcile competing demands whilst protecting the interests of local people. Most structure plans, local plans and UDPs outline policy and strategy on the protection and enhancement of landscape character, provision of recreation facilities and the use of green-space.

In some areas local authorities have produced indicative forestry strategies and community woodland plans which link in with existing development plans and indicate areas with most potential for the expansion of forestry and the creation of community woodlands.

## Landscape protection and enhancement

In the UK, highly distinctive regional landscapes have evolved over the centuries in response to the influences of climate, geology and patterns of land use. These landscapes are under increasing pressure, particularly on the urban edge, due to human pressure, changing land use patterns and the high cost of maintaining landscape features that no longer serve a practical function. With improving communications and mass production, regionally distinctive landscapes are being homogenised by a standardisation of materials and design in the land based industries. This influence is increasing as the means have become more readily available to modify patterns of land use on a large scale, for example through hedgerow removal, opencast mining and trunk road construction.

In some areas local landscape patterns are being analysed as a basis for strategies to protect and strengthen them. Because trees are a key component of the landscape, landscape assessments are being increasingly used as the basis for planning the extent, design and character of woodland planting around towns. Where large scale planting is planned, for example in the designated community forest areas, landscape assessments are of key importance in promoting the balanced expansion of woodland cover which is sensitive to landscape heritage and current demands on land. Price (1993) presents a framework for carrying out landscape assessments.

## Providing a recreation network

Urban woodlands will be most valuable when they form part of an interlinking network of foot paths, cycle ways and recreational features. Concentrate effort and resources on planting that will strengthen existing features and that will be accessible from rights of way. The ideal is to work towards a skeleton of greenways – paths and tracks running from the heart of towns and cities into the countryside, flanked by woodlands and green-space designed to provide opportunities for recreation and amenity and to enhance the landscape viewed from the rights of way. Canals, river courses and disused railways offer good possibilities for forming the basis of such a network.

## A long-term perspective

When planning for woodland creation or management you must consider the availability of time, commitment, expertise and resources. The fact that woodland is a long-term land use is often not recognised in resource allocation and staff responsibili-

Plate 2.2 The desire for instant impact often results in negative impact.

Plate 2.3 A heavily used urban woodland in need of a programme of management. (*40960*)

ties and, furthermore, the responsibility for wood land and trees can be shared between different departments and individuals. The increasing use of contractors adds further links to the chain of management. The essential ingredients of practical planning, sensitive implementation and a commitment to long-term management can only be secured by coordinated teamwork between landscape designers, experienced foresters and enlightened resource managers on the basis of clearly defined responsibilities.

The way in which local authorities and other agencies are financed, along with a common desire for instant impact, often results in generous short-term funding for tree and woodland planting with little or no resourcing for essential long-term care and maintenance. An increasing emphasis on the planting of new woodlands could further divert resources from the management of existing woodlands. This leads to a decline in the quality of the woodland estate as a whole and increases the risk that today's newly planted woodland will become tomorrow's neglected woodland. The first priority must be management of existing woodlands for these reasons:

- The greatest short-term gain in public benefits from woodland comes from bringing existing derelict woodlands into management.

- Unmanaged woodlands may still have considerable value for landscape, recreation and wildlife but continued neglect can result in rapid decline. Neglected woodlands attract antisocial activities, are prone to windthrow, often contain dangerous trees, lack regeneration of the species required to perpetuate the wood, and are likely to suffer a decline in wildlife value because of shading, people pressure and reducing structural diversity.

- Well-managed existing woodlands will foster a positive attitude towards increasing woodland cover (and towards the agency trying to achieve it).

Most new woodlands can be planned to yield produce whatever their main objectives, and the financial return will increase the scope to manage woodlands in a planned and sustained way. For wood to be marketable there must be enough of a uniform product to interest a buyer (Chapter 8, Woodlands for timber production). Consider designing small woodlands to fit in with a wider working plan which allows a viable annual harvest. Coppice has great potential for integrating sustainable wood production for local use with amenity, landscape and community involvement objectives if managed in this way.

## Grants and advice

The Woodland Grant Scheme, administered by the Forestry Authority, is the principle source of grant aid for urban woodland establishment and management. New planting and restocking or regeneration after felling are currently eligible for planting grants, and for woodlands to be planted within five miles of urban areas a substantial supplement may be available for actively encouraging public access. Planting on arable land and improved grassland is currently eligible for another supplement. For established woodlands, annual management grants are available where there is an agreed five-year management plan.

Tree planting on farms may be eligible for annual payments for up to 15 years under the Farm Woodland Premium Scheme, in addition to Woodland Grant Scheme grants. The Farm and Conservation Grant Scheme offers 30% grant aid on shelterbelts, hedges and enclosure of grazed woodland to exclude stock.

Derelict Land Grant is funded by the Department of the Environment and administered by English Partnerships and the Welsh Development Agency for the reclamation of 'land so damaged by industrial or other development that it is incapable of beneficial use without treatment'. Tree planting may be grant aided where:

- development of the site is not imminent;
- trees offer the most cost effective treatment;
- the treatment significantly improves the demand for the site;
- trees are likely to be a permanent feature of the site;
- where the trees will be largely visible to passers by.

Levels of grant range from 50 to 100% of approved costs, depending on location and ownership. The Department of the Environment manages other urban regeneration grants, currently including City Grant and City Challenge, all of which may grant-aid tree planting as part of derelict site redevelopment. Derelict Land Grant is to be subsumed by the Single Regeneration Budget in 1996, which will also incorporate City Grant, English Estates, the Coalfield Areas Fund, the Urban Partnership Fund and the urban development corporations.

In Scotland, Derelict Land Grant is not available but Local Enterprise Companies are involved in restoring derelict land.

## Additional grants for amenity woodlands

- Some local authorities offer grant aid for local small scale tree and hedgerow planting schemes.

- The Countryside Commission Countryside Stewardship Scheme is designed for the conservation and development of chalk and limestone grassland, lowland heaths, waterside landscapes, coastal areas and moorland in England. Where tree planting is planned as part of a stewardship agreement grant is paid at a fixed rate per tree. This scheme will be administered by the Ministry of Agriculture, Fisheries and Food from 1995. Countryside Commission landscape conservation grants are administered by local authorities and the amount of grant aid given is at the discretion of the local authority tree officer.

- English Nature offers conservation grants for a wide range of practical projects of benefit to nature conservation. English Nature Community Action for Wildlife grants are offered to enable community groups to carry out activities that will benefit wildlife and the local community. English Nature school grants are given to help schools create opportunities for wildlife within their grounds.

- The Countryside Council for Wales has a whole farm scheme, Tir Cymen, which offers annual payments for positive management of natural features and for providing new opportunities for people to enjoy the countryside. In addition, the Landscape and Nature Conservation Grant Scheme is administered through the county councils and grants are available for urban forestry projects and programmes.

- Scottish Natural Heritage gives grant aid for small-scale tree and hedge planting projects, generally administered by local authorities.

- The European Union may be a source of grant aid in certain parts of the country under the European Regional Development Fund, the European

Social Fund, and funds for the improvement of run down ex-coal mining, ex-shipbuilding and ex-steel industry areas (RECHAR, RENAVAL, RESIDER).

- The Department of the Environment Local Action Fund, administered by the Civic Trust.
- Training and Enterprise Councils.
- Scottish Enterprise.
- The Sports Council.
- Tourist boards.
- The Tree Council.
- The Prince of Wales Committee.
- Trusts, hundreds of which allocate funds for environmental activities.

Advice on woodland creation and management is available from the Forestry Authority and all Forestry Commission publications referred to in this Handbook can be obtained from the Forestry Commission's Publication Section. Some local authorities have woodland or tree officers, and community and urban forest projects give advice within their project areas. The Black Country Urban Forestry Unit is increasingly providing urban forestry advice on a national basis. The Arboricultural Advisory and Information Service gives advice on amenity tree planting and management, and forestry or arboricultural consultants offer a range of services and skills. The Institute of Chartered Foresters and the Arboricultural Association maintain registers of consultants.

## Sponsorship for tree-related activities

Raising money and funding in kind is a major part of the work of urban and community forest initia-tives, and some local authorities are looking for additional resources for woodland work.

Securing sponsorship is a form of trading. The company or organisation interested in sponsorship will want the benefits from their involvement to be greater than the cost of sponsorship. The benefits sought are usually publicity, 'green' image building and contact with a target audience. The demands of a sponsor may not always be compatible with the approach that the urban forestry project would like to take and the negotiated compromise represents the cost of the deal to the urban forestry project. Funding in kind is often the best way to maximise benefits to both parties. The sponsor may provide land for planting, trees, ground preparation equip-ment, etc. or make available staff or skills. In this way, the real cost to the sponsor is small compared to the value to the recipient and this, in turn, means that the sponsor requires less return on the invest-ment. Take care when considering deals: a seeming-ly generous offer may become counter-productive if the sponsor tries to dictate the identity of the project.

Urban and community forestry projects are, by nature, environmentally oriented and geographical-ly defined. Local companies are likely to see bene-fits in linking their name to a local 'green' initiative. Some national companies are dedicated to helping environmental projects and have set up specific ini-tiatives to help dispense aid such as the Shell Better Britain Campaign, Ford British Conservation Awards, Forte Community Chest and Barclays Youth Action.

## Urban woodlands and the law

### Responsibilities to site users

The occupier of a site has a duty to visitors, under the Occupiers Liability Act 1967, 'to take such care as is reasonable to see that the visitor is reasonably safe in using the premises for the purpose for which he is invited or permitted to be there'. The duty owed to different classes of visitor will vary and the occupier must expect that children will be less careful than adults. This liability was extended in 1974 to include uninvited visitors. There is an exclusion in the legislation for organised educational parties.

## Safe working practices

Under the Health and Safety at Work Act 1974, both employers and employees have a duty to ensure health, safety and welfare at work for themselves and others. Where contractors or volunteers are invited onto a site to undertake work, the person in control of the 'non-domestic premises' has responsibility to ensure that the premises, access, egress and articles or substances provided for use there are safe.

A range of safety guides covering most woodland operations is available from the Forestry and Arboriculture Safety and Training Council and the Health and Safety Executive. Use them to ensure safe working practices, and keep a record of safety checks that you do and the action taken to reduce risks and make safe hazards.

## Pests

Landowners have a duty (under the Pests Act 1954, Agricultural Act 1947 and Agricultural (Scotland) Act 1948) to control rabbits and vermin on their land if they are interfering with the use of neighbouring land or (under the Forestry Act 1967) if they are damaging trees. Under the Weeds Act 1959 occupiers of land have a duty to control the spread of spear thistle, creeping thistle, curled dock, broadleaved dock and ragwort from their land, and under the Wildlife and Countryside Act 1981 it is

an offence to allow Japanese knotweed and giant hogweed to grow in the wild.

## Tree preservation orders

Local planning authorities can protect trees, stands of trees and woodlands using tree preservation orders (TPOs). This prohibits the cutting down, lopping, uprooting or wilful damage of trees except with the consent of the local planning authority, and may require replanting of woodland felled as part of a TPO permission. Woodlands that are covered by a Forestry Authority Woodland Grant Scheme plan of operations are exempt from TPO restrictions.

## Felling licences

A felling licence is normally required from the Forestry Authority to fell growing trees more than 8 cm in diameter. If a licence is refused the owner may be entitled to compensation. A licence is not required for work to prevent danger or abate a nuisance, for the felling of trees in compliance with a statutory requirement, at the request of an electricity company, for development authorised by planning permission, or if felling is in accordance with an approved plan of operations under one of the Forestry Authority's grant schemes.

## Trees and boundaries

Land managers have certain obligations in respect of boundaries with neighbouring land and highways. Boundary trees must not cause undue nuisance to neighbours by overhanging branches or unreasonable reduction in light to adjacent properties. The neighbour is entitled to cut back branches to the boundary and may seek an injunction for the reduction in size of trees blocking light. There is no right in law to a view and obscuring a view by planting trees cannot be legally regarded as a nuisance. If the roots of trees on one property cause damage or nuisance to the owner of an adjoining property (for example subsidence of a building on shrinkable clay), the owner of the tree may be liable for damages. Landowners who plant poisonous trees, such as yew, near a boundary and allow the branches to grow, or leaves to blow, over their neighbours' land are liable if the neighbours' animals suffer as a consequence.

# For more information

## Publications

The Arboricultural Association. *Directory of consultants and contractors.* Ampfield House, Romsey, Hampshire, SO51 9PA. (01794) 368717.

Department of the Environment (1992) *Circular 29/92: Indicative forestry strategies.* HMSO, London.

Directory of Social Change. *A guide to major trusts and raising money from trusts.* Radius Works, Back Lane, London, NW3 1HL.

Harris, J. G. S. (1991). *Trees and the law.* The Arboricultural Association.

The Institute of Chartered Foresters. *List of members in consultancy practice.* 7A St. Colme Street, Edinburgh, EH3 6AA. (0131) 225 2705.

Lorrain-Smith, R. (annually updated). *The Calderdale grants for trees booklet.* Calderdale Metropolitan Borough Council, Leisure Services Department.

Price, G. (1993). *Landscape assessment for indicative forestry strategies.* Forestry Authority England, Cambridge.

Scottish Development Department (1990). *Indicative forestry strategies.* Circular 13/1990.

Shell Better Britain Campaign. *Getting help for community environmental projects.* Red House, Hill Lane, Great Barr, Birmingham, B43 6LZ.

## Advice

The Arboricultural Advisory and Information Service, Alice Holt Lodge, Farnham, Surrey, GU10 4LH. (01420) 22022.

The Black Country Urban Forestry Unit, Red House, Hill Lane, Great Barr, West Midlands, B43 6LZ. (0121) 358 1414.

The Community Forest Unit, Countryside Commission, Fourth Floor, 71 Kingsway, London, WC2B 6ST. (0171) 831 3510.

Countryside Commission, John Dower House, Crescent Place, Cheltenham, Gloucestershire, GL50 3RA. (01242) 521381.

Countryside Council for Wales, Plas Penrhos, Ffordd Penrhos, Bangor, Gwynedd, LL57 2QL. (01248) 370444.

Department of Agriculture for Northern Ireland, Dundonald House, Newtownards Road, Belfast, BT4 3SB. (01232) 520000.

English Nature, Northminster House, Peterborough, PE1 1UA. (01733) 340345.

Forestry Authority England, Great Eastern House, Tenison Road, Cambridge, CB1 2DU. (01223) 314546.

Forestry Authority Scotland, Portcullis House, 21 India Street, Glasgow, G2 4PL. (0141) 248 3931.

Forestry Authority Wales, North Road, Aberystwyth, Dyfed, SY23 2EF. (01970) 625866.

Forestry & Arboriculture Safety & Training Council, 231 Corstorphine Road, Edinburgh, EH12 7AT.

Forestry Commission Publications Section, Alice Holt Lodge, Farnham, Surrey, GU10 4LH. (01420) 22255.

Health and Safety Executive, Library and Information Services, Broad Lane, Sheffield, S3 7HQ.

Ministry of Agriculture Fisheries and Food, Nobel House, 17 Smith Square, London, SW1P 3HX. (0171) 238 3000.

Scottish Natural Heritage, 12 Hope Terrace, Edinburgh, EH9 2AS. (0131) 477 4748.

Scottish Office Agriculture and Fisheries Department, Land Use Branch, Pentland House, 47 Robb's Loan, Edinburgh, EH14 1TW. (0131) 556 8400.

Welsh Office Agriculture Department, Subsidies and Lands Branch, Trawsgoed, Aberystwyth, Dyfed, SY23 4HT. (01974) 261301.

# 3 Working with local people

## Why work with local people?

It is a paradox that the publicly owned urban forest has traditionally been managed with little input from the public themselves. This may be because involving local people in urban woodlands is time consuming and the benefits are often hard to measure. So, why bother with community involvement? The answer to this question lies at the heart of what urban forestry is all about: to benefit urban people, not just by improving their living environment, but also by offering the power of involvement and encouraging active citizenship. An urban woodland initiative can become a focus for the development of communities and individuals, and the project team should be concerned with nurturing local communities as well as with nurturing trees.

**There are real benefits to community involvement in urban forestry.**

- Allows conflict to be anticipated, defined and resolved at an early stage.
- Increases responsiveness to local needs and desires.
- Engenders a positive image for an initiative.
- Harnesses the ideas, commitment, energy and expertise of local people.
- Builds links between the 'authorities' and local people.
- Helps reduce vandalism in local woodlands.
- Raises local support which can influence potential funding agencies and sponsors.
- Fosters a greater awareness, appreciation and sense of responsibility for trees and the natural environment.
- Through increasing understanding and involvement, results in greater support for forestry throughout the UK.

## Building links with the local community

The first step in the process of community involvement is to define the relevant communities. There are two principle types: communities of neighbourhood and communities of interest.

Where the focus of community involvement is a particular site then an approach to the community of neighbourhood will usually be most appropriate. This community is defined entirely geographically as those people who live around and use the site and there will often be no other community bond within this group. The principal interest of these people will be how the site can be managed to meet their needs and desires. One important role of community woodland initiatives is to draw local people together by this common focus and so, out of passive communities of neighbourhood, create active and fulfilling communities of common interest around a woodland site.

For community forestry initiatives set up on a town or city scale, community involvement in the initiative is best developed through communities of interest (Table 3.1). Each community of interest

Plate 3.1   If local people can be enthused about a
particular site, a new community of interest can be
created with opportunities for fun and friendship.

**Table 3.1   Examples of communities of interest**   (adapted from the Countryside Commission advice manual for the preparation of a community forest plan).

**Landowning**

| | |
|---|---|
| Landowners and occupiers | Private and public.  LAs, CLA, BC, BR, FC, EN, DOT, NT. |
| Farmers | Land owning and tenant.  NFU, FWAG, YFC. |
| Woodland interests | Land owning and tenants.  FC, Woodland Trust, NT, LAs. |

**Business**

| | |
|---|---|
| Local businesses | Local companies and national companies.  CBI, Rotary clubs, chambers of commerce. |

**Citizens**

| | |
|---|---|
| Local environment | Residents' associations, parish councils. |
| Sport | e.g. Anglers' Federation, local fishing clubs, British Horse Society, local riding clubs, orienteering clubs, motor scrambling clubs. |
| Leisure | e.g. Regional arts associations, painting clubs, Ramblers' Association. |
| Community farms | NFCF, local city farms. |
| Wildlife | Urban wildlife groups, county trusts, watch groups, RSPB, local natural history societies. |
| General environment | e.g. FOE, Groundwork Trusts, BTCV, CPRE, civic trusts, amenity societies, environmental networks. |
| Education | PTAs, school clubs, WEA groups, universities. |
| Children | Pre-school groups, schoolchildren, youth groups. |
| Women | WI, Townswomen's Guild. |
| Ethnic groups | Black Environment Network. |
| Disabled groups | Fieldfare Trust. |
| Senior citizens' groups | |
| Religious groups | |

BC – British Coal; BR – British Rail; BTCV – British Trust for Conservation Volunteers; CBI – Confederation of British Industry;
CLA – Country Landowners' Association; CPRE – Council for the Protection of Rural England; DOT – Department of Transport;
EN – English Nature; FC – Forestry Commission; FOE – Friends of the Earth; FWAG – Farming and Wildlife Advisory Group;
LAs – Local Authorities; NFCF – National Federation of City Farms; NFU – National Farmers' Union; NT – National Trust;
PTAs – Parent Teacher Associations; RSPB – Royal Society for the Protection of Birds; WEA – Workers' Education Association;
WI – Women's Institute.

Plate 3.2  The main types of community of interest are a) landowning (*E8463*); b) business; and c) citizens. (*41046*)

will have a different focus and different reasons for being willing to get involved with community forestry. The approach to each community of interest is best tailored to make clear how its involvement and support is relevant to its interests as well as to those of the initiative.

Some communities of interest are relatively easy to access. For example, schools, conservation volunteers, scouts and guides are often keen to play a role in a new project, especially where it is tailored to meet a specific interest such as the national curriculum or local historical ecology. Other communities are much more difficult to access and may feel remote from the countryside, preoccupied with daily necessities such as employment or health and cynical about money spent on what they perceive as low priorities. Making the project relevant to them is a greater task and requires patience, persistence and commitment. In the urban fringe many people are not active citizens and are not affiliated to any community of interest. These are the most difficult people to get involved, but as support grows through contact with communities of interest, it will become easier to motivate unaffiliated residents into involvement. Identification of key opinion formers can be a gateway into inaccessible communities.

A supply of land is critical for the creation of community woodlands, particularly in the urban fringe where landowners hope to develop agricultural and vacant land. With the policy of achieving new community woodlands by voluntary incentive, the farming and landowning community is a most important community of interest. Farmers and landowners are often understandably cautious about allowing access to land where crops and livestock may be at risk. If positive relationships can be fostered between them and neighbouring residents, more progress may be made in releasing land for new community woodland.

---

**In order to succeed in building links with the local community an urban woodland initiative must:**

- understand people's need for a feeling of relatedness to others and to the life of the community;
- be proactive in order to build positive links with local people;
- foster a down-to-earth local image with which local people can identify – a glossy, high profile, civic dignitary, photo-opportunity approach can alienate local people;
- extend a sense of identity into a sense of ownership – if people feel they have a personal stake in a project they will be motivated to help it succeed; and
- have a long-term outlook – building up community involvement is about building relationships and earning people's trust: this takes time.

---

## The nature of community involvement

Community involvement includes any activity in which local people are actively considered as part of the woodland management process (Figure 3.1). The ladder of participation defines the spectrum of community involvement from creating and managing woodlands *for* local people, through creating and managing woodlands *with* local people, to helping local people create and manage woodlands *for themselves*.

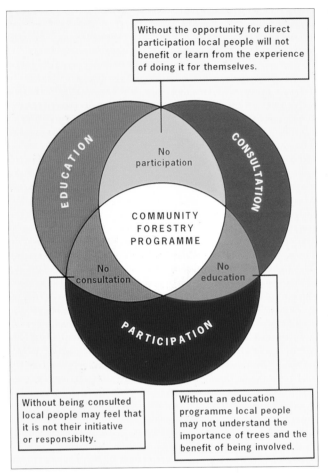

Without the opportunity for direct participation local people will not benefit or learn from the experience of doing it for themselves.

No participation

EDUCATION

CONSULTATION

COMMUNITY FORESTRY PROGRAMME

No consultation

No education

PARTICIPATION

Without being consulted local people may feel that it is not their initiative or responsibilty.

Without an education programme local people may not understand the importance of trees and the benefit of being involved.

Figure 3.1 The aspects of community involvement required for a successful community forestry programme.

If you want to involve the local community at all, it is important to find out at an early stage how much involvement local people want. This must then be reconciled with the ability, objectives and resources of the agency or landowner. Don't assume you know what local people want; ask

them. Views on the appropriate extent of community involvement may develop over time and so goals should be periodically reviewed. Be aware, though, that trying to whip up involvement beyond the desire of local people can alienate the community and appear patronising.

The 'top down' approach, where an agency or landowner tries to generate community involvement, is most vulnerable to failure. Most examples of successful community involvement have been initiated by local people and related to specific needs in the local environment. Agencies must foster enthusiasm in the local community for environmental improvement and local woodlands which will hopefully result in the community deciding to get involved and then approaching the agency for help. This sort of community-led involvement is most likely to meet the needs of local people.

## Information and education

Providing information is the first step towards full participation and can be done at two levels.

- **Educational information** raises people's awareness of the contribution and benefits of trees in the urban environment. For example, a project may need to help local people appreciate the difference between neglect and low level management. Nature is often untidy and many people who are brought up to expect a neat and tidy city landscape do not initially appreciate the informal appearance of thriving naturalistic habitats in towns.

- **Site-based information** on projects under way in the locality increases the interest of local people and reduces negative attitudes. Dissemination of this information will be most intensive in the

## The ladder of participation

| | |
|---|---|
| Community control | The community is in full control of a scheme and makes the decisions regarding resource allocation, use and management. Agency involvement is available, but at the direction of the group. |
| Community participation | The community is undertaking substantial aspects of the community woodland programme without significant input from the agency. The agency is increasingly taking a back seat and a local group may have formed to formalise community involvement. |
| Community involvement | Members of the community who have become interested through consultation are encouraged by the agency to become involved with appropriate aspects of the planning, implementation and management of the community woodland scheme. |
| Consultation | Members of the community are actively encouraged to offer ideas and options that can be incorporated into the scheme if appropriate. |
| Information | Telling people what is going to happen without recruiting support or offering the opportunity to comment. |
| Persuasion | Securing a commitment to an objective of community involvement and a structure to achieve it within the agency. |
| Agency control | A scheme is provided by the agency or landowner with no actual or intended reference to the community. |

locality of the scheme and may take the form of leafleting, an article in the local press, or unmanned displays in the local school, library or supermarket. It is important to present information in a lively and interesting way, making the most of points of human interest like historical connections with the site and cultural associations with the tree species.

Plate 3.3 Involving children with urban woodlands offers many educational opportunities and formative experiences.

Woodlands offer a wide range of educational possibilities for pre-school, primary and secondary schools, colleges, adult classes and interest groups.

- School competitions, inviting designs for a woodland, suggestions for a name, posters, essays or poems on what it could be like. Winning entries can be used.
- School adoption of plots in the woodland for planting, managing and monitoring trees and for teaching, celebration and adventure play.
- Developing work sheets around a specific woodland to cover aspects of natural history, biology, environmental education, history and maths (Figure 3.2).

An example of the guidance available on using trees and woodlands in schoolwork is provided by Clark and Walters (1992).

Figure 3.2 An example of the development of an education resource alongside a community woodland project.

# COST AND BENEFITS OF PLANTING OAKS OF DIFFERENT SIZES

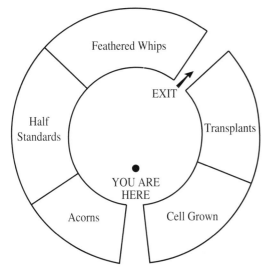

Feathered Whips

EXIT

Half Standards

Transplants

YOU ARE HERE

Acorns

Cell Grown

## BROADFIELDS FARM
DEMONSTRATION WOODLAND

## Tasks

1. Measure the total height of the labelled trees in each sector.
2. Plot the heights on the histogram below (Column B).
3. Calculate the increase in height from November 1991 and plot this growth on the histogram (Column C).
4. Calculate the cost of each sector and fill in the boxes below the histogram (the cost of each tree is on the signs, there are 16 trees in each sector).
5. Why do you think Thames Chase usually plants transplants?

6. Estimate how long it will take for the transplants to 'overtake' the half standards.

A = Height at planting (November 1991)   B = Present height (April 1993)   C = Growth

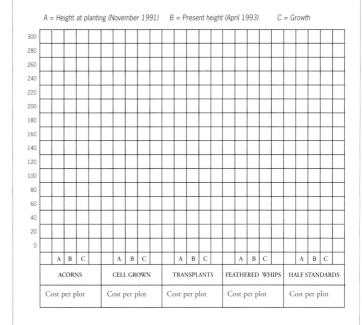

| | ACORNS | | | CELL GROWN | | | TRANSPLANTS | | | FEATHERED WHIPS | | | HALF STANDARDS | |
|---|---|---|---|---|---|---|---|---|---|---|---|---|---|---|
| A | B | C | A | B | C | A | B | C | A | B | C | A | B | C |
| Cost per plot | | | Cost per plot | | | Cost per plot | | | Cost per plot | | | Cost per plot | | |

25

# Consultation

Consultation is the process of actively seeking an input of ideas and views before plans are fixed. How you consult depends on what you want to consult about and on the target audience. Don't, for example, hold an evening meeting in an area where some people are afraid to go out after dark. Successful consultation encourages local people to express their views without feeling 'put on the spot'. Consultation must relate the proposals in a way appropriate to the audience, and the opinions and comments of local people must be recorded. People need to know that their views and ideas are being taken seriously and will be used where possible. It is important to make clear the aims of consultation so that people do not commit themselves to a level of involvement they cannot sustain.

| Appropriate forms of consultation | Less appropriate forms of consultation |
|---|---|
| **Working groups** with invited representatives from the various communities of interest can be more productive than public meetings. If nurtured, groups may become involved in the implementation and management of woodland schemes and may eventually be encouraged to take a lead in running the site. | **Public meetings** may be well attended where contentious issues have arisen. However, an ongoing commitment to public consultation should prevent such issues from gaining prominence as they tend to generate negative feeling and prevent a proactive approach. In practice, most public meetings to discuss urban woodland development are poorly attended and the people that do attend can have extreme and polarised views. |
| **Manned displays** in public places can be an effective means of soliciting public comment on a proposal, particularly if the display material is lively and the approach is not intimidating. | **Postal questionnaires** rarely result in a full and balanced response and are not effective at establishing contacts with local people. |
| **Site meetings** with local people promote discussion over proposals for a site. Plan site meetings with a core of invited community representatives but extend the invitation to all-comers through local publicity. | **Comments by post** from community representatives do not help in building contacts with local people and written responses are usually less forthcoming than verbal ones. |
| **Person to person** questionnaires can be good as a straw poll of local preferences and to establish a dialogue with local people. However, the results of a questionnaire will vary greatly depending on where and when it is carried out. | |

Visual props make consultation more interesting and help people decide on their views. Remember though that many people find it difficult to understand maps or interpret complicated diagrams. Here are some suggestions for attractive material.

- Panoramic diagrams of the proposed woodland from key viewpoints.

- Models of the proposed woodland or, better still, hands-on models that allow different options to be explored (Plate 3.4).

- Comment cards and box that allow people to identify problems and potential solutions. Anonymity is preserved, allowing creative inputs even from those who don't normally like to speak in public meetings.

- Display boards showing options for the objectives (Plate 3.5) or the appearance of a scheme (Plate 3.6), using stick-a-dots to allow people to express their preferences.

Plate 3.5 Design for a display board with possible objectives for a proposed woodland. People put black stick-a-dots against their first choice, and red stick-a-dots against their second choice.

Plate 3.4 Visual props can bring the process of consultation alive. This tree planting model allows trees to be inserted by consultees.

Plate 3.6 Design for a display with options for the appearance of a proposed woodland. Stick-a-dots are put against the preferred option.

However it is done, it is important to recognise that consultation is the key to providing local people with the woodlands that they want, as well as a way of drawing people into full participation in urban woodland projects. Without arranging a mechanism for consultation, the progression from *working for*, to *working with* local people cannot be achieved.

## Participation to benefit local people

As a result of providing information, educating and consulting, some local people will be keen to become more involved with your woodland project. Community involvement describes the involvement of people in activities planned and organised *for* them, whereas participation describes the involvement of people in activities planned and organised *with* them. Involvement must come before participation in order to create interest, overcome apathy, inspire ideas and show people the benefits of being involved. The move towards greater participation can be achieved only by gradual delegation of tasks as and when volunteers are ready to accept greater responsibility, not by a sudden withdrawal of professional help.

There are two main sources of volunteers:

- people from the local community can be time consuming to recruit and achieve little on the ground, but are most likely to offer a long-term commitment to the project;
- volunteers recruited through an umbrella organisation such as BTCV tend to be easier to enlist, and groups often come with their own leader, equipment and experience – they are a good way of getting a job done but not of generating long-term commitment to a project.

People volunteer for many and varied reasons and thus bring with them many expectations. But, always remember that the primary reasons why most people become involved in this sort of activity are to have fun and meet people.

Plate 3.7  Improving and creating wildlife habitats is a popular form of participation in environmental work.

**Activities around which community participation events can be organised**

**Seed collection and tree nurseries.** Collecting and growing seed from local woodlands or notable trees is a good way of establishing a link between the existing tree resource and proposed new woodlands.

**Tree planting** has to take place in winter which is not a popular time for events and is likely to be attended only by specifically invited groups or particularly committed volunteers unless other attractions can be provided.

**Participation in aftercare.** Involvement in tree planting should, if possible, be followed up by participation in aftercare activities. Encourage local people to help with mulching, fertiliser application, litter picking and other maintenance activities. Establishing a continuity of involvement on a site will help to foster the sense of community ownership and demonstrate the whole process of woodland creation.

**Providing for wildlife.** Activities such as pond creation and bird or bat box making and erection provide some of the most appealing opportunities for enjoyable public participation, but generally require a considerable amount of organisation both before and during the event.

**Managing existing woodland.** Activities based in existing woodlands are good for encouraging local people to get involved: established woodlands are generally attractive places to spend some time and there is potential for the results of the work to be immediately obvious. Scrub clearance, glade creation, coppicing and footpath maintenance are the most common activities. If the task is large chainsaws and clearing saws should be used, but only by trained operators.

**How to get the best out of *volunteers* and give back a rewarding experience**

- Ensure that the job of work is of real value to the environment and the community. Volunteers soon lose heart if they are just being used as cheap labour.
- Ensure that the reasons for the work and the methods of carrying it out are clearly explained. Many volunteers are keen to learn.
- Safety is paramount. Ensure the right equipment is provided and correct procedures are followed.
- Do not overwork people; let them work at their own speed and at jobs they feel capable of doing.
- Encourage people to contribute their own ideas and experiences to the project and, where appropriate, let them take responsibility, for example by leading the group.
- Provide training for suitable volunteers. As well as teaching skills, this increases confidence and self-esteem.
- Provide rest breaks and refreshments, and say 'Thank you'.

Voluntary warden schemes are a good way of getting local people involved in woodlands as they offer responsibility and a measure of prestige to volunteers, and therefore often result in a long-term commitment.

## Organising events

Before organising an event define the target audience, so that the details and publicity can be appropriately tailored. A good turn out is most likely if the event is organised around an invitation to a particular community of interest such as a school or community group, with wider publicity extending an open invitation. This reduces the risk of poor attendance, which can be a discouragement to those who do attend as well as a poor return on the effort of organisation.

Plan events to maximise the enjoyment and satisfaction of volunteers. Encourage a relaxed informal atmosphere, for instance, by taking group photographs, providing refreshments, or having a bring-your-own barbecue. At key events the effort of organising demonstrations, community artists, musicians or displays may be worth while to maximise local interest. Allow volunteers to help themselves to woodland produce as an additional reward for involvement.

As your initiative develops, the need for special events to engender support should become less as local people become involved on a regular basis, their efforts being channelled through local groups set up to manage specific sites or to service particular interests and needs.

## Tips for a successful event

- Start planning at least three months ahead.
- Ensure the availability of key groups when setting the date.
- Choose weekends between 10.00 am and 4.30 pm but avoid bank holidays and peak holiday periods when many people will have made other arrangements.
- Make sure you have the necessary permissions for working on the site and inform or invite neighbouring residents.
- Establish clearly who has responsibility for organising particular aspects of the event. Ensure the availability of skilled supervisors and project staff known to local groups.
- Trees, tools, skips, etc. must be organised up to two months ahead.
- Arrange first aid cover and insurance. Volunteers working should be covered by public liability insurance (to at least £250 000) for any damage or injury they may cause to property or to the public. Individual cover against personal accident is also advisable for regular volunteers.
- Organise publicity for the week before the event. Consider leafleting, posters and using local newspapers, although the importance of personal invitations and word of mouth should not be underestimated. Any publicity material should include information on the location of the event, suitable clothing and any need to bring tools or refreshments.
- The site should be well organised and prepared in advance of the event, ensuring that the work area is free from hazards and that ample parking is available. Take account of restrictions such as rights of way and wayleaves.

# For more information

## Publications

Clark, R. and Walters, P. (1992). *Trees in the school grounds.* Learning Through Landscapes Trust, Third Floor, Southside Offices, The Law Courts, Winchester, Hampshire, SO23 9DL. (01962) 846258.

Davidson, J. (1990). *Advice paper 6: Involving local communities.* In: Advice manual for the preparation of a community forest plan. Countryside Commission, 19–23 Albert Road, Manchester, M19 2EQ. (0161) 224 6287.

Kiser, B. (1991). *Trees and aftercare: a practical handbook.* BTCV, 36 St Mary Street, Wallingford, Oxfordshire, OX10 0EU.

Shell (1989). *Making community action work in the environment.* Report of a workshop at Losehill Hall, December 1988. Shell Better Britain Campaign.

## Advice

The Community Development Foundation, 60 Highbury Grove, London, N5 2AG. (0171) 226 5375.

The Community Forest Unit, Countryside Commission, Fourth Floor, 71 Kingsway, London, WC2 B6ST. (0171) 831 3510.

# 4  The right specification

The failure of many urban woodlands can be predicted, even before they are planted, from the nature or lack of any specification.  A comprehensive specification for the period from site preparation to the end of the establishment phase, along with the design plan, is essential to ensure that your scheme is suited to the site and the uses to which it will be put.  The steps needed to get the best woodlands on the ground are shown in Figure 4.1.

## Is woodland the best use of the site?

Before deciding to plant woodland on a site ask these questions.

- Will the site support woodland?
- Will woodland add to the value of the site?

- Could tree planting adversely affect the site?
- Are there any legal, contractual or statutory constraints on tree planting?

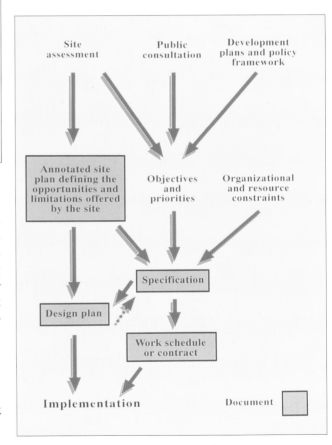

Figure 4.1 Elements in the process of planning urban woodlands.

## Will the site support woodland?

Some urban and degraded sites will not support healthy tree growth due to extremes of pH, electrical conductivity or toxicity, or abundance of rubble or stone. The minimum soil standards acceptable for woodland planting are shown in Table 4.1. The site must support trees not only during the establishment phase, but on to maturity if a valuable woodland resource is to be created. If a site is not capable of supporting tree growth to maturity after appropriate ground preparation, then woodland should only be planted if reclamation works are undertaken.

Planting trees that fail either to establish or achieve the objectives of planting will undermine your credibility and require the repayment of grant aid. If you have any doubts about the potential for woodland establishment get expert advice from a forestry consultant (Chapter 2, Grants and advice).

Plate 4.1  Will the site support woodland?  The effect of extreme acidity on the vegetation of this colliery spoil site should have alerted those planning tree planting to the problem. (*40974*)

### Table 4.1  Minimum soil standards for tree establishment on disturbed land (from Moffat and Bending, 1992)

| | |
|---|---|
| Depth | Not less than 1 m of rootable soil material[1] |
| Bulk density | <1.5 g cm$^{-3}$ to at least 50 cm depth<br><1.7 g cm$^{-3}$ to 1 m depth |
| Aeration status[2] | Soil oxygen >5% during the growing season |
| Stoniness | <40 % by volume; few stones greater than 100 mm in size |
| pH | 3.5–8.5 |
| Electrical conductivity | <2000 µS cm$^{-1}$  (1:1 soil:water suspension) |
| Iron pyrite content | <0.5% |
| Heavy metal content | Not excessively over ICRCL[3] threshold trigger concentrations |
| Organic contaminants | Not exceeding ICRCL[3] action trigger concentrations |

1  1.5–2.0 m of soil recommended on modern landfill sites where cap forms part of the pollution control measures.
2  Particularly relevant to landfill sites.
3  Interdepartmental Committee on the Redevelopment of Contaminated Land.

## Will woodland add to the value of the site?

In some situations openland provides valuable benefits. The site may support rare openland plant or animal communities that would decline under the shade of trees. The site may be heavily used and greatly appreciated by local people as it is. Some sites have a long history as open commonland or heathland, and may contain features of archaeological value. In some circumstances, maturing trees may cause a nuisance to surrounding landowners or residents.

## Could tree planting adversely affect site quality?

Tree planting will only very rarely have any adverse effect on site quality, but theoretical risks include:

- the uptake of contaminants by tree roots, their movement to the foliage and eventual deposition onto the soil surface at leaf-fall;
- the acidification of a contaminated substrate by prolonged tree growth, and the consequent increase in contaminant solubility and mobility;
- the penetration, or drying and cracking, of poorly engineered caps designed to cover and seal contaminated materials or landfill; and
- the possibility of windthrow exposing an engineered cap or contaminated materials at the soil surface.

## Are there any legal or contractual constraints on tree planting?

Constraints may be imposed by:

- landscape, conservation or heritage designations
- existing management agreements
- planning permissions
- wayleaves for overground or underground cables and pipes

- conditions attached to the title deeds
- commoners' rights.

## Site assessment

Before you can formulate the specification and design you must get to know the site. Verbal and written descriptions and photographs may be useful, but there is no substitute for getting out onto the site and digging holes in it. Site assessment should include:

- site history
- existing woody vegetation
- existing ground vegetation
- characteristics and variability of soil-forming materials
- evidence of damaging agents
- exposure and frost
- surrounding land uses
- existing uses of the site
- features of archaeological or cultural value
- landform and visual analysis.

For each aspect of the analysis consider strengths, weaknesses, opportunities and threats (SWOT). Annotate a site plan with your findings as a basis for drafting the specification and preparing the landscape design (Figure 4.1).

### Site history

This will give clues as to what site constraints or problems can be expected. For example, former industrial land may be affected by toxic materials, poorly restored sand and gravel workings may be prone to drought stress and infertility, cultivation of abandoned farm land may lead to an explosion of

Plate 4.2 Site assessment is the essential first step in formulating a specification for woodland creation.

arable weeds, and colliery spoil may be affected by extreme acidity.

## Existing woody vegetation

Existing trees and shrubs should be retained wherever possible. Not only does existing woody colonisation give the planting scheme a head start, but species composition and spatial distribution are often appropriate to the character of the area (Chapter 6, Natural colonisation). On the other hand, existing woody vegetation can be a problem if it is profuse and of species incompatible with long-term objectives.

## Existing ground vegetation

Ground vegetation should be assessed for three reasons.

- To identify species and habitats of conservation value. Valuable grassland and openland plant communities of importance are not uncommon on vacant urban land. The chemical constituents and physical structure of soil-forming materials on some derelict sites can result in habitats similar to semi-natural ecosystems such as coastal grassland, downland or heathland. A local authority ecologist or local conservation group may be able to survey potentially interesting sites and advise on the value of the ground vegetation.

- The distribution of ground vegetation will highlight parts of the site where soil conditions are particularly inhospitable. Site history may indicate possible reasons such as the presence of toxic substances, extremely low moisture-holding capacity, extreme infertility or barriers to rooting (e.g. concrete below the surface).

- The range of species present must be taken into account when deciding on the most appropriate method of weed control around the newly planted trees.

## Soil characteristics and variability

Assessing soil-forming materials helps to determine whether the site has the capacity to support trees and is essential for decisions on the need for ground preparation (Table 4.1). Most planting sites will need amelioration of site physical conditions and some will also need amelioration of site chemical conditions. The assessment of site physical conditions can be routinely undertaken without expert assistance but if you suspect chemical contamination seek expert help.

Because of the variability of many urban sites, soil-forming materials should be assessed systematically across the site and with particular intensity on areas of sparse ground vegetation. Dig soil pits of 70 cm depth to assess compaction, drainage and the presence of rubble and stone. Visual assessment may be all that is needed to identify soil physical

**Table 4.2 Indications of the need to apply fertiliser from soil analysis**

|  | Probable need | Possible need | No need |
|---|---|---|---|
| Extractable P (mg per litre) | 0–9 | 10–15 | 16+ |
| Extractable K (mg per litre) | 0–60 | 61–120 | 121+ |
| Extractable Mg (mg per litre) | 0–25 | 26–50 | 51+ |

problems, but compaction can be more accurately assessed by using a penetrometer or taking bulk density samples.

Soil samples should be analysed for phosphorus (P), potassium (K), magnesium (Mg) and pH – a standard analysis available at low cost from laboratories undertaking analysis of agricultural soils. Table 4.2 shows the likely need for fertiliser from soil analysis, although the interpretation of soil analyses cannot be hard and fast because of the effect that other site characteristics can have on essential element availability. Nitrogen is difficult to assess in soils and is not generally included in analyses, but on most disturbed, non-agricultural sites nitrogen is in short supply.

Poor soil physical conditions can prevent the uptake of essential elements and cause trees to be deficient even when soil analysis indicates that levels in the soil are sufficient. If this is suspected, foliar analysis (which can include nitrogen) of woody vegetation on site may be more revealing (Table 4.3). With non-agricultural substrates assess soil conductivity, as high conductivity can damage and kill newly planted trees.

Plate 4.3 Incorporation of this naturally colonised hawthorn into the woodland design will offer elements of instant woody structure. (*41102*)

Plate 4.4 Methane seepage on this landfill has killed all vegetation on some parts of the site.

**Table 4.3 Deficient and optimal foliar nutrient concentrations (% oven dry weight) (from Taylor, 1991)**

|  | Nitrogen | | Phosphorus | | Potassium | |
|---|---|---|---|---|---|---|
|  | def. | optimum | def. | optimum | def. | optimum |
| Ash | <2.0 | >2.3 | <0.19 | >0.22 | <0.7 | >0.9 |
| Beech | <2.0 | >2.3 | <0.14 | >0.16 | <0.7 | >0.9 |
| Birch | <2.5 | >2.8 | <0.19 | >0.22 | <0.7 | >0.9 |
| Common alder | <2.5 | >2.8 | <0.16 | >0.18 | <0.7 | >0.9 |
| Corsican pine | <1.2 | >1.5 | <0.12 | >0.16 | <0.3 | >0.5 |
| Larch | <1.8 | >2.5 | <0.18 | >0.25 | <0.5 | >0.8 |
| Norway maple | <2.0 | >2.3 | <0.19 | >0.22 | <0.7 | >0.9 |
| Oak | <2.0 | >2.3 | <0.14 | >0.16 | <0.7 | >0.9 |
| Sweet chestnut | <2.0 | >2.3 | <0.14 | >0.16 | <0.7 | >0.9 |

*Notes*
Values are tentative for species other than Corsican pine.    Values between deficient and optimum are described as marginal.

**Table 4.4 Maximum acceptable concentrations in parks, playing fields and open space for heavy metals (from Moffat and McNeill, 1994)**

| Contaminant | Threshold concentration (mg per kg air dried soil) |
|---|---|
| Contaminants which may pose hazards to health | |
| Arsenic | 40 |
| Cadmium | 15 |
| Chromium (hexavalent)[1] | 25 |
| Chromium (total) | 1000 |
| Lead | 2000 |
| Mercury | 20 |
| Selenium | 6 |
| Contaminants which are phytotoxic but not normally hazardous to health | |
| Boron (water-soluble)[2,3] | 3 |
| Copper[2,4,5] | 130 |
| Nickel[2,4,5] | 70 |
| Zinc[2,4,5] | 300 |

*Conditions*

All values are for concentrations determined on spot samples based on adequate site investigation carried out prior to development. They do not apply to analysis of averaged, bulked or composited samples.

If values are above the threshold, remedial action may be needed.

1 Soluble hexavalent chromium extracted by 0.1M HCl at 37°C; solution adjusted to pH 1.0 if alkaline substances present.

2 The soil pH value is assumed to be about 6.5. If the pH is lower, the toxic effects and the uptake of these elements will be increased.

3 Determined by standard ADAS methods (soluble in hot water).

4 Total concentration (extractable by $HNO_3/HClO_4$).

5 The phytotoxic effects of copper, nickel and zinc may be additive. The threshold values given here are those applicable to the 'worst case'; phytotoxic effects may occur at these concentrations in acid, sandy soils. In neutral or alkaline soils phytotoxic effects are unlikely at these concentrations.

If you suspect that toxic substances are present, detailed soil analysis will be needed. Site history will give clues to the substances present. Soil-forming materials on certain industrial sites, some types of mine spoil, and land that has received heavy doses of sewage sludge in the past may need analysis for a range of heavy metals. A typical analysis would include lead, cadmium, copper, nickel, zinc, chromium, mercury and arsenic. The recommended safety limits for these metals (Table 4.4) are lower than the levels that are phytotoxic and so it is these safety limits that should be considered as the maximum. Some industrial sites may warrant analysis for organic contaminants such as diesel, or toxic manufactured compounds.

## Damaging agents

Evidence can often be found on site to indicate the types of damage likely (Table 4.5). The risk of damage by cattle and sheep should be predictable and, in certain parts of the country, informal horse grazing is commonplace and to be expected. Local foresters, farmers, rangers or estate managers may be useful sources of information on the local status of deer which can cause serious damage by bark stripping and browsing. Hares tend to frequent open agricultural land and are most often to be seen during the spring.

Evidence of rabbits should be reasonably obvious on the site or surrounding land from burrows, scrapes, droppings, areas of tightly grazed sward, gnawing around the base of trees and browsing damage to small trees. Rabbit populations have returned to pre-myxomatosis levels in many areas and it is best to assume that protection will be needed unless site inspection clearly indicates other-

**Table 4.5   Identification of bark stripping and browsing damage on young trees (adapted from Kerr and Evans, 1993)**

| Mammal | Tree size | Time of year | Description of damage |
|---|---|---|---|
| **Bark stripping** | | | |
| Field voles | Young trees to 5 cm diameter | All year but greatest risk in winter | Bark is stripped on the roots or lower stem up to the height of surrounding vegetation from where the attack is carried out. Very small trees can be girdled and felled. Bark is usually removed in short, irregular strips 5 to 10 mm wide, with incisor marks 1 mm wide in pairs. |
| Rabbits | All | Winter and spring | Bark stripping can occur to a height of 55 cm (higher in snow). Incisor marks are 3 to 4 mm wide, in pairs, usually running diagonally across the stem. |
| Deer | Pole stage | All year | Red, sika and fallow deer strip bark leaving vertical incisor marks. Bark fraying results when male deer rub new antlers to remove velvet and mark territories. |
| Livestock | All | All year | Severe stripping of bark to the height of the livestock type. Intensity of stripping often leads to tree death. |
| **Browsing** | | | |
| Rabbits | | Winter/spring, occasionally summer | Sharp angled cut on the ends of stems or branches, removed portion usually eaten. Damage occurs to 50 cm, or higher during snow. |
| Hares | | As rabbits | As rabbits but shoots are not consumed. Damage can be up to 70 cm. |
| Deer | | Mid November to spring | Lack of teeth in front upper jaw produces a ragged edge on damaged stems. Roe and muntjac to 1.1 m, fallow and red to 1.8 m. |
| Livestock | | Summer | Coarse browsing of foliage to 2.5 m with horses, 2.0 m with cattle and 1.5 m with sheep and goats. Newly planted trees can be pulled out of the ground. |

wise. The risk from field voles is more difficult to assess as evidence of their presence on the unplanted site may not be obvious, and populations tend to be cyclical, often increasing rapidly after a mild winter. Evidence of voles includes gnawing around the base of young trees, vole runs in grass and holes in the ground about 2 cm across. High vole populations are most likely in areas of rank grass.

People can be the most serious damaging agents on urban planting sites. Vandalism, fire-raising, motorcycle scrambling and fly-tipping can be serious problems but are often localised. Evidence of these activities must strongly influence the planting specification and implementation strategy.

## Exposure and frost

Wind damage to trees is more prevalent in the lowlands than commonly supposed, especially in flat landscapes devoid of hedgerows and trees or on prominent sites like spoil mounds. Wind affects trees during the establishment phase by causing socketing in the soil at the base of the stem, which damages roots and makes the trees unstable. Treeshelters will be blown over on windy sites unless firmly staked. Windthrow of maturing trees can devastate a woodland. The risk is highest on exposed sites with shallow or compacted soils which restrict the depth of rooting. On these sites take particular care to achieve a full one metre depth of rootable material.

Frost is a particular problem on flat or concave sites where frost pockets readily form. The most damaging frosts occur during early autumn, when trees are not fully hardened off, and especially during late spring as trees start to break bud and flush. On frost-prone sites even normally hardy species such as ash and lime can be badly affected by

Plate 4.5 Late frosts can be a serious limitation to the establishment of some species, such as this Norway spruce. (*8821*)

Plate 4.6 The prominence of housing next to this planting site necessitates careful design to minimise the negative impact of the woodland on local residents, and minimise the negative impact of the housing on woodland users. (*41103*)

dieback each year, and so a proportion of particularly hardy species should be used.

## Surrounding land use

Surrounding land uses will affect the type of people using the wood, what they want to do in the wood, and how long they want to stay. For example, woodland near housing is most likely to be used for dog walking and children's play whereas woodland near commercial areas may be used for short cuts to work and lunch-time relaxation. Factors such as local parking facilities and links with rights of way will also affect patterns of use. Also assess the landscape impact of surrounding land uses. Woodlands can be designed to provide a valuable buffer to existing development and eyesores, whilst maintaining existing fine views from within the woodland.

### Existing uses of the site

Current users will want to continue to use the site after woodland planting. If their activities are not antisocial they should be accommodated as far as possible. The woodland design must allow for the continued use of existing paths and access points. Failure to appreciate the desires of existing site users undermines the reason for providing urban woodland on the site – to benefit the public – and may result in vandalism.

### Features of archaeological or cultural value

Records held by local authorities will usually indicate the presence of known archaeological features. On sites that have not been greatly disturbed in the recent past it may be worth inviting the local authority or local history society archaeological expert to survey the site before ground preparation begins. Historical and past industrial associations with a site are often less tangible but can be, nonetheless, important to local people. Sympathy towards, and allusion to, such associations in the woodland design can help to create a spirit of place which is lacking in many new urban and urban edge woodlands.

### Landform and visual analysis

Much of the landscape design process involves recognition and analysis of landscape components. To do this you need some understanding of visual design principles relating to shape, visual force, scale, diversity, unity and spirit of place. Assess the landform and other visual aspects of the site and surrounding landscape with these design principles in mind. Visit prominent view-points from which the site is visible and take photographs which will be useful for developing the landscape design (Chapter 9, The landscape design plan). The

Forestry Commission's *Forest landscape design guidelines* describe visual design principles and how to undertake a site visual analysis as a basis for the landscape design.

## Setting objectives and priorities

Site assessment will define the limits to what is silviculturally possible and visually acceptable for a site. Within these limits the woodland design should cater for the uses to which the site will be put. Many schemes are planted with no particular end use in mind and the resulting woodlands, whilst filling up vacant space and creating incidental benefits, do not contribute to urban amenity as much as they could. For most urban woodlands there will be a number of objectives, commonly including landscape enhancement, amenity and recreation, habitat creation and wood production. For publicly owned sites, these objectives must be defined and accorded priority in the light of:

- information derived from the site assessment;

- the views of local people (Chapter 3, Consultation); and

- development plan policies and commitments (Chapter 2, Development plans).

As well as setting broad objectives, consider the specific uses likely to be made of the woodland as these will influence the detail of design and highlight areas of potential conflict. Make sure that objectives reflect primarily the needs and desires of local people rather than the convenience of managers and officials.

Objectives should be clearly written into the specification. Woodland is a long-term land use and written documentation may be the only thread

The clear definition and ordering of objectives creates a benchmark against which to assess the scheme, allowing:

- a focus on the specification and design considerations appropriate for different end uses;
- an assessment of the feasibility of the specification needed to satisfy the desired objectives: if the scheme is not feasible due to budgetary or site constraints, the objectives should be re-defined;
- a comparison of costs against the likely benefits of the scheme (over and above the costs and benefits associated with the site in its current state);
- an objective assessment of the success of the scheme: it is only by such assessment that skills and experience in urban woodland establishment and management can be built up; and
- conflict between objectives to be resolved by clear ordering of priorities: in situations where objectives are likely to conflict (for example, where visitor pressure may limit wildlife value), clearly defined priorities will identify which objective must be compromised (in the example above, either controlling access to visitors or accepting a reduction in wildlife value).

of continuity between a succession of site managers. The woodland design can then be formulated, in the light of the specification, to achieve these objectives.

There are two approaches to designing multi-purpose woodlands.

- Designing for the range of objectives to be fulfilled on the same piece of land.
- Zoning.

Some objectives are easily compatible on the same piece of land, such as landscape enhancement and informal recreation, but some uses are not compatible and need separating. In small woodlands this may mean, for example, designing to encourage people to stay on the paths to protect nature conservation interests in other parts of the site. Large woodlands can be more fully zoned, with a different primary objective for each zone. Careful woodland design and management can help to contain site users within the appropriate zone without resorting to barriers and 'Keep out' signs.

## The importance of robustness

Few woodlands are more difficult to establish than those on degraded, heavily used, urban sites. Careful management minimises tree losses but to reduce the risk of failure a robust specification is needed that takes into account the vulnerability of woodlands during the establishment phase, and the effect that this can have on tree survival and growth. The creation of robust woodlands should be considered in two stages.

1. Creating a woodland environment: the specification for woodland establishment.
2. Satisfying woodland-based objectives: the management of the established woodland.

### Creating a woodland environment

Whatever the objectives of a scheme, the first prerequisite is the successful establishment of trees.

Plate 4.7  Low initial stocking reduces the chances of creating a woodland environment.

You will usually want to create a woodland environment as quickly as possible, to minimise the period until the realisation of objectives and to minimise the vulnerable establishment phase. The most practical way of creating robust woodlands is to use an approach based on sound silvicultural practice (Chapter 5) that meets the biological needs of the trees, anticipates and minimises likely losses and hence maximises the probability that woodland will be created.

Creating a woodland environment does not mean planting trees on every available part of the site. Site assessment will indicate areas that should be left unplanted because of valuable light-demanding plant communities, existing paths, recreational needs and particular view points.

## The robust approach to urban woodland creation

| | |
|---|---|
| Ground preparation | Soil compaction reduces tree survival and growth. Compaction must be relieved over the whole site, usually by ripping. |
| Species choice | Whether native or introduced, species must be suited to site conditions. |
| Species mixtures | Simple mixtures of compatible species are appropriate for informal woodlands and are practical to plant and manage. |
| Planting stock | Small, sturdy forestry planting stock tends to survive and grow better than large stock sizes. |
| Tree spacing | Sufficient trees should be planted to result in full stocking at the end of the establishment phase. Planting should be at 1.5 × 1.5 m on difficult sites, 2.0 × 2.0 m on good sites. |
| Planting | Small planting stock can be notch planted into well-prepared ground. |
| Tree protection | Effectively excludes, or protects trees from, the mammal pest species present. On heavily used sites protection should not restrict access or draw attention to the trees. |
| Weed control | In lowland Britain competition for moisture is the main limitation to successful tree establishment. Maintenance of weed-free conditions around the base of the tree for five years greatly improves survival and growth. |
| Vegetation management | Vegetation between weeded spots need not be regularly mown. Mowing is expensive, damages trees, makes planting stock more vulnerable to vandalism and reduces natural informality. |
| Fertiliser | Spot-applied fertiliser, in combination with effective weed control, can boost the growth of newly planted trees on nutrient deficient sites. |

By anticipating losses, the robust approach to woodland establishment:

- can prevent failure of the woodland when losses occur;
- creates a mutual nursing effect, the trees sheltering each other and encouraging good height growth;
- reduces the need for beating up (replacing of dead trees);
- minimises the duration of the vulnerable establishment phase;
- can create useful, functioning woodlands in as little as three years; and
- maintains the choice of management options for the satisfaction of woodland-based objectives.

**Satisfying woodland objectives**

The quality of the tree resource at the end of the establishment phase will dictate the scope of management options for satisfying woodland objectives. The options available will be greatest on a well-stocked site, as it is much easier to remove unwanted trees than to establish additional trees. On poorly prepared and poorly stocked sites the only realistic options are to start again or to compromise the objectives of the scheme by managing the area as open ground with scattered trees and scrub.

If woodland establishment using the robust approach has been successful and survival is good, the detail of the design can be implemented by tree removal. The timing of intervention and the number of trees to be removed will depend on the objectives of the woodland and the success of establishment. By not being too rigid about the layout of open space at planting, areas of persistently poor establishment can be used as open space without reducing the wooded area beyond what was originally planned.

## Drafting a specification

The two stage approach to woodland creation should be reflected in the specification.

1. Prepare the specification for woodland establishment well before planting.
2. Prepare the first five-year plan for the subsequent management of the woodland (Chapter 7, The management plan) towards the end of the establishment phase.

The package of information needed for the creation of a new urban woodland will generally come in three parts:

- the written specification;
- the map-based design and layout; and
- the work schedule for tree establishment.

The draft written specification, developed on the basis of the site evaluation exercise, forms the framework for the design plan and contract documents, although as the design of the woodland develops the written specification may need to be amended. The written specification is your record of site information, the objectives of woodland creation and your vision for the woodland, and is the best way to ensure clear communication. Without the written specification plans will lack purpose, management will lack direction and woodlands will not achieve their potential.

## Practical woodland design

The landscape design should be based on the draft specification and the site assessment. It should show how the objectives for the woodland can best be met in the light of the constraints and opportunities presented by the site, and organisational and resource constraints. The most important design

**Essential elements of a woodland specification**

1   Site name, location and grid reference.

2   Identification of project coordinator.

3   Brief background to project – why the site is available for planting, organisations or parties involved, context of any local initiatives, development plan commitments, etc.

4   Objectives of woodland planting on the site, listed by priority.

5   Site description: include information on size of the site, site history and ownership, existing woody
vegetation, existing ground vegetation, substrate type, results of soil analysis, existing features on the site, evidence of damaging agents, evidence of exposure, surrounding land use, existing uses of the site, wayleaves, designations, other constraints to management, and hazards to safe working (using maps as appropriate).

6   Rationale for planting – woodland type or types (high forest, coppice, coppice with standards, wood pasture), species mix for each distinct part of the woodland, the characteristics desired of each distinct part of the woodland.

7   Silvicultural details – prescriptions for ground preparation, species choice and mixture, planting stock type, tree spacing, planting methods, tree protection, duration and timing and type of weed control, management of inter-row vegetation, fertiliser application, and beating up.

8   Open space – objectives and management prescriptions for open space within the wood.

9   Timing – deadlines for major operations leading up to and including planting should be detailed.

10  Responsibilities – clear definition of responsibilities in the specification can avoid misunderstandings during implementation.

11  Resource requirement – numbers of trees of each species, type and length of fencing, area requiring ground preparation, herbicide and fertiliser requirement.

12  Review dates: review progress and achievement after planting and at the end of the proposed period of weed control. Setting review dates:
    • gives an opportunity to revise the specification;
    • highlights lessons to be learnt from the implementation of the specification; and
    • prompts you to formulate the first five-year managment plan for the established woodland.

13  Distribution list: distribute the final specification to all parties involved with, or affected by, the proposal. Recording the distribution of the specification makes the circulation of revisions and subsequent management plans easy.

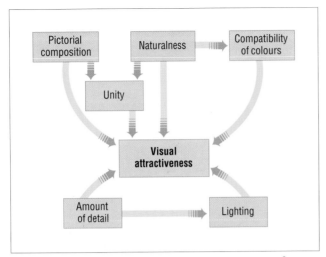

Figure 4.2 Relationships between various aspects of the environment and its visual attractiveness (from Arboricultural Association, 1990).

considerations for creating visually attractive woodlands have been determined by a consumer preference study (Figure 4.2). Ways to design visually attractive woodlands that can also perform other functions are shown in the Forestry Commission's *Community woodland design guidelines, Lowland landscape design guidelines,* and *Forest landscape design guidelines* which cover landscape assessment, visual design principles, detailed design elements, design of open space, woodland design for mineral workings and derelict land, and design for informal recreation.

This section focuses on the reconciliation of woodland design with the practical aspects of implementation, a process which is essential if designs are to result in successful woodland on the ground. Chapter 8 considers design aspects for particular woodland-based objectives.

## Design with scale in mind

The scale of many urban woodlands falls between the detailed 1:500 approach of many landscape architects and the extensive 1:10 000 scale of many foresters. When the 1:500 approach is applied to sites of over one hectare the result is complicated designs that are difficult and expensive to implement, and possibly not the most appropriate to the site. Conversely, sites planned using the 1:10 000 approach may lack the detail required to ensure that specific points of design importance are implemented. A successful design should work at all scales. To achieve this, resolve the landscape scale issues first and then move to progressively finer detail.

One of the benefits of urban woodland is natural simplicity which must be balanced against the benefits of diversity. The key to achieving this balance is to understand that the impact and value of diversity depends entirely on the scale at which it is planned. A woodland comprising an intimate mixture of 20 species over the whole site will appear monotonous to many site users and will provide little visual diversity or additional interest as the user walks through the wood. More effective is to create areas of planting that are relatively simple but which contrast with each other to provide a diversity of experience over the whole site. For example, a path might run from an area of predominantly oak high forest, through a glade into hazel coppice with oak standards, up a slope skirting the edge of an area of larch high forest, fringed with birch, rowan and scattered oak established on poorer soil.

## Design with robustness in mind

The need for robust urban woodlands has implications for species choice and woodland design. On many urban sites, inhospitable substrates and people pressure can rule out a total reliance on the

Plate 4.8  Using an alder 'skeleton' to add robustness
to a vulnerable urban woodland. (*40977*)

species that would be preferred and result in a need to plant at least a proportion of particularly tough species.

On the most difficult sites it must be accepted that tolerant species are the only ones likely to establish successfully. A 15- to 30-year rotation of tolerant species may improve the site sufficiently to allow replanting with preferred species, particularly if coppice regrowth can be used to nurse the newly planted trees.

On less severe sites, a design incorporating a framework of tolerant species within a matrix of preferred species will add robustness to the woodland. If the preferred species establish successfully, the tolerant ones can be gradually removed after the establishment period. If the preferred species fail then the tolerant ones will, at least, create the appearance of woodland cover on the site, and offer a later opportunity to replant the preferred species in sheltered conditions. Because of the difference in likely growth rates between tolerant and preferred species it is usually better to plant them in separate blocks, rather than in intimate mixture (Chapter 5, Species mixtures).

## Design with timescale in mind

Woodland is a long-term land use. While the formulation of a design must be undertaken well before planting, the implementation of that design should span the period from the first site preparation operation to woodland maturity. A common mistake is to try to complete the implementation of a design at planting, which results in a lack of robustness and increases the risk of failure. Although a design is created with the mature wood-

---

**Implementing a woodland design**

- **Before planting.** The broad layout of the woodland types and access points and paths will be marked out on site.

- **At planting.** The species mix will be implemented.

- **During the establishment phase.** Beating up can be used to adjust and diversify the species mix. Differential fertilizer regimes can encourage the development of naturalistic woodland edge. The instigation of ride mowing regimes will encourage the development of the desired ground vegetation structure. The detail of the design will be adjusted around areas of poor tree establishment.

- **Soon after the establishment phase.** Coppicing may be initiated in parts of the wood. Vigorous tolerant species should be removed if directly competing with less vigorous preferred species. Additional shrub planting around glades and woodland edges may be beneficial.

- **In the maturing woodland.** Management may be required to maintain fine views out of the wood. Selective felling and restocking may be desirable to increase structural diversity. Coppice rotations will be established and the size, shape and order of cutting determined. Ride widening may be needed to maintain sunlit conditions in the rides. Trees may need to be cut back from ponds or streams.

Plate 4.9 This planting scheme used 21 species, mostly in intimate mixture. This has led to a fussy appearance and lack of natural simplicity. (*40967*)

land in mind, it will be appropriate to implement specific aspects of the design at different stages in the development of the woodland.

## Design with implementation in mind

A robust woodland design must take into consideration the skills and resources available for implementation and subsequent management. Over-ambitious or complicated designs and maintenance requirements are expensive, difficult to implement, and can result in fussy looking woodlands. The most complicated designs are usually the least likely to succeed.

## Design to minimise vandalism

Community involvement in the planning and implementation of a scheme can do much to reduce vandalism and antisocial behaviour. Another key to successful urban woodland provision is to under-

stand the causes of antisocial behaviour and to create woodlands in a way that minimises it.

- People do not like change when it is imposed on them (whether for the better or the worse). The robust approach minimises the impact of the change of land use from open land to woodland. However, when woodland is to be planted into mown sward the impact of change can still be great. Consider delaying planting for a year and leaving the areas to be planted unmown as an intermediate stage between intensively mown grass and extensively managed woodland.

- Some people tend to be negative towards 'the authorities'. Imposed schemes can be seen as legitimate targets on which to vent frustrations. The robust approach, if implemented sensitively, is perceived by local people to be more a result of the natural processes of growth and tends not to attract this sort of attention.

- People feel antagonistic if their use of the site is interrupted. The woodland design should accommodate existing uses of the site, paths (Plate 4.10) and access points where possible. If possible find an alternative site for inappropriate activities such as motorcycle scrambling or informal horse grazing.

- High impact schemes have a high challenge value to vandals. The vandal's efforts are prominent with big trees at wide spacings (Plate 4.11) and the satisfaction of causing damage is high in the knowledge that the trees were costly. Efforts to protect big planting stock against vandalism further increase the challenge and hence the determination of the vandal. Small planting stock minimises the challenge value of new planting and minimises the cost consequence and impact of vandalism that does occur. Where serious van-

Plate 4.10  Strong desire lines on planting sites should be incorporated into the woodland design.

Plate 4.11  The challenge and satisfaction of vandalising prominently planted large stock is high. Forestry type planting could reduce the incidence of vandalism and have a dramatic effect on the amenity value of the site.

dalism is anticipated use species that will coppice vigorously if broken off.

- Failing, neglected planting schemes are seen as a legitimate target for vandalism, tipping and other forms of depreciative behaviour. The robust approach should result in healthy, vigorous woodland which is less likely to attract significant vandalism.

- The robust approach reduces the need for expensive, high-input management but the evidence of carefully targeted management (such as weed control around trees) should be clear so that site users do not interpret low-input management as neglect.

## Work schedules and contracts

The work schedule is derived from the specification and gives detailed instructions to the operatives planting the woodland. The use of contractors to undertake forestry work is now commonplace and so the work schedule often takes the form of a contract. If work is to be undertaken in-house or by volunteers, the preparation of a work schedule can still be valuable in clarifying details of the work programme.

The balance between rigid instructions and performance specification in the work schedule depends on the capability of the operatives. A performance specification details the final outcome that is required (for example, a 1 m × 1 m area at the base of each tree should be kept 80% weed-free between the beginning of April and the end of September) but leaves the method of achieving it to the discretion of the operatives. This allows the detail of operations to be modified in response to prevailing circumstances and site and weather conditions, makes the most of operatives' skills and knowledge, and so can result in a lower price and a better job.

The use of contractors can offer flexibility in work programming and can encourage the development of a woodland skills base in urban areas where there is no tradition of woodland establishment and management. The contract should include the first two or three years of maintenance as well as planting, offering an incentive to the contractor to maximise the quality of the initial planting operation in order to minimise the cost of subsequent tree replacement.

There are four main ways of letting contracts.

- **Negotiation.** A contract is agreed through direct negotiation with an individual contractor. Negotiation is most appropriate for small or complicated jobs where the preparation of tender details would not be justified, and where known and trusted contractors are available. Use negotiated contracts to foster new and small contracting firms, or to try out an unknown contractor on a small job.

- **Single tender.** A schedule of work is supplied to a single contractor who returns a written quote for the job. Using single tender contracts requires knowledge of the going rate for the job as the lack of competition may result in a high price. Contracts can be set up quickly by single tender, but the lack of competition makes it suitable only for small jobs using known and trusted contractors.

- **Selected tender.** A limited number of contractors are invited to tender for a job. For a large work programme and where you know of a number of contractors, selected tenders usually attract the lowest prices, whilst limiting the time and expense of setting up the contract. The work schedule and conditions of contract must be clear and comprehensive so that returned, priced tenders are fully comparable. Make sure to give new contractors the opportunity to tender.

- **Open tender.** An intention to let work is advertised giving any contractor an opportunity to tender. In some organisations all jobs over a particular value must go to open tender. The cost of advertising and the lead time required before work can start can be offset by lower prices.

Open tenders are a good way to evaluate the contractor resource in an area, or to draw in contractors from further afield for particularly large jobs.

The objective of multiple tender is to maximise the cost effectiveness of a work programme but this does not necessarily mean accepting the lowest tender.

- Is the tender price unrealistically low?
- Does the contractor have the necessary skills to undertake the work?
- Is the contractor likely to deliver the quality of work required within the specified time?

The need for clarity throughout a work schedule and contract document cannot be overemphasised. Whatever type of contract is used, hold a site meeting with the prospective contractor(s) before a deal is struck to ensure that the work schedule and contract conditions are understood. The contractor will have the opportunity to explain problems arising from the work schedule and to suggest practical modifications. Site meetings and regular contact with contractors and their operatives will help to ensure that the contract achieves its objective: the creation of healthy and vigorous urban woodlands.

Plate 4.12 There is no substitute for all parties involved discussing plans on site.

## Outline of a woodland planting and maintenance contract

In Chapter 9, The tree establishment contract section shows the conditions of contract for the planting of Freckland Wood.

**Instructions to tenderers.** This outlines the procedure for tendering.

**Preliminary particulars.** Will include the name, location and a brief description of the site, a brief description of the type and extent of works, details of access to the site, and a key to site plans.

**General conditions of contract.** Many organisations have their own standard conditions of contract. Additional conditions, such as limitation of working hours, protection of services, laying and removal of temporary hard-standings, protection of existing trees, and reporting of archaeological finds, may be required for certain works or sites.

**Specific conditions of contract.** A set of standard specific conditions can be drawn on as necessary for each individual contract. Specific conditions will vary according to the job, but will commonly include guidance on:

- acceptable conditions for site preparation
- specification for fencing, stiles and gates
- approved suppliers of plants
- quality, handling and inspection of plants
- method of setting out the site
- acceptable conditions for planting
- preferred method of planting
- planting of mixtures
- beating-up surveys
- timing and quality of weed control
- control of noxious weeds
- ride management and grass cutting
- fertiliser application
- removal of litter
- requirement for site meetings.

**Schedule of work and bill of quantities.** Gives work details that are particular to the site including the quantity and description of materials, such as plant numbers and the length and type of fencing. The schedule should make clear whether materials are to be supplied by the contractor, the employer or a third party; the required breakdown of costs; and critical work deadlines. This part of the schedule can be simplified with reference to standard specific conditions.

**Schedule of payment**. Should detail the arrangements for payment.

**Maps and site plans.**
- Site location map.
- Site plan detailing the design of the scheme and the location of the various operations.
- Site plan indicating access points for the contractor, any constraints or hazards on site such as overhead or underground services and, if appropriate, where stores or other buildings may be located.

## Model contract conditions for use in urban forestry contracts.

This agreement is made between (name of client) (hereinafter called 'The Client') and (name of individual or firm) (hereinafter called 'The Contractor').

The contractor hereby agrees to carry out the work specified in the first schedule attached hereto, to the satisfaction of the client subject to the following terms and conditions.

1. **Preliminary arrangements.** The client will enable the contractor to commence prescribed operations on the dates scheduled and give him such instructions and advice as affect the contract.

2. **Work sites and access.** The contractor will familiarise himself with work sites and the authorised access routes. The use of such access routes shall be at the contractor's own risk and the client shall not be responsible for any damage or injury arising out of the contractor's use of such routes.

3. **Payment.** The client will pay the contractor the agreed price for the specified work provided that it has been completed to the client's satisfaction. By mutual agreement, payment may be made in instalments not in excess of the value of the work completed. Ten percent of sums due will be retained from all invoices to be paid on satisfactory completion of the contract. In the event of the contractor failing to complete any part of the work to the client's satisfaction, the client may declare this agreement void (insofar as it relates to such part of the work), and payment shall only be made for any portion of that work certified as fit for payment. The contractor shall compensate the client for any additional expenditure incurred as a result of his failure to complete the work satisfactorily.

4. **Liability.** The contractor will indemnify the client against any claims for loss, injury or damage occasioned by the act of default of the contractor in the execution of this agreement, and will if so requested, satisfy the client that he is adequately insured.

5. **Force Majeure.** In the event of any government regulation or departmental order coming into operation, or any act of God, strike, lockout or any other occurrence of a serious nature beyond the control of the contractor taking place, affecting their ability to perform their obligations under the agreement and as a result of which the work detailed hereof is delayed or suspended, either party may request an alteration to the period of the agreement.

6. **Rewards.** The contractor shall not offer any reward, prerequisite or emolument whatsoever to any person in the employment of the client.

7. **Health and Safety at Work Act 1974.** The contractor will accept full responsibility for compliance with the Health and Safety at Work etc. Act (1974), and all other relevant Acts and Regulations in respect of the work comprised in the contract and taking place within the land, access routes or other premises of the client. In the event of any breach in these standards committed by the contractor, sub-contractor or his employees or agents then he will be informed of the nature of the breach and of the remedial action to be taken within a specified time. Failure to meet the conditions imposed within the time specified shall be regarded as a breach of contract.

8. **Precautions.** The contractor shall take all reasonable precautions to prevent a nuisance or inconvenience to the owners, tenants or occupiers of other properties and to the public generally.

9. **Assignation.** The contractor shall not sub-let or assign his rights under this contract except with the written consent of the client and upon such terms as the client may require.

10. **Suspension of work.** The contractor shall at the direction of the client suspend or delay work on the whole or part of the contract, if in the opinion of the client such suspension is necessary, and shall recommence such work within three days of the client's written order to do so. If in the opinion of the client such suspension is due to circumstances which could not have reasonably been foreseen by the contractor, the client may authorize reimbursement of any increased cost which in their opinion the contractor has incurred.

11. **Termination.** If the contractor commits a serious breach of any of the terms or conditions of this contract, the client shall have the right by written notice to require the contractor to remedy the matter within 14 days, and if the matter is not so remedied the client shall have the right to terminate the contract, and any termination shall be without prejudice to the client's other rights or remedies under the contract.

12. **Removal from site.** The contractor shall within one month of the termination of the contract remove from the site any equipment or erections belonging to him. Should the contractor fail to remove any such equipment or erections within the time specified, the client may retain or remove them as he thinks fit, and the contractor shall on demand re-imburse the client for all costs incurred in their disposal after receiving credit for any value which the client has placed upon them.

13. **Settlement of disputes.** If any dispute or difference of any kind shall arise out of any of the provisions of the contract upon which agreement cannot be reached between the client and the contractor, the dispute or difference shall be referred to an independent arbitrator agreed upon between the parties for a decision. Which decision shall be final and binding upon the parties.

Date:

Signed:                                Contractor.

Signed:                                On behalf of the client.

# For more information

## Publications

Arboricultural Association (1990). *Amenity valuation of trees and woodlands.* Ampfield House, Romsey, Hampshire, SO51 9PA.

Binns, W. O., Insley, H. and Gardiner, J. B. H. (1989). *Nutrition of broadleaved amenity trees: 1. Foliar sampling and analysis for determining nutrient status.* Arboriculture Research Note 50/89/SSS. Arboricultural Advisory and Information Service, Farnham.

Bridges, E. M. (1987). *Surveying derelict land.* Clarenden Press, Oxford.

British Standards Institution (1988). *DD 175: Code of practice for the identification of potentially contaminated land and its investigation.* BSI, London.

Dobson, M. C. and Moffat, A. J. (1993). *The potential for woodland establishment on landfill sites.* HMSO, London.

Forestry Commission (1994). *Forest landscape design guidelines.* HMSO, London.

Forestry Commission (1992). *Community woodland design guidelines.* HMSO, London.

Forestry Commission (1992). *Lowland landscape design guidelines.* HMSO, London.

Gilbert, O. L. (1989). *The ecology of urban habitats.* Chapman and Hall, London.

Institute of Chartered Foresters (1992). *List of members in consultancy practice.* 7A St Colme Street, Edinburgh, EH3 6AA.

Interdepartmental Committee on the Redevelopment of Contaminated Land (1987). Guidance on the assessment and redevelopment of land. ICRCL *Guidance Note 59/83.* DoE Publications Sales Unit, Building 1, Victoria Road, South Ruislip, Middlesex, HA4 0NZ.

Joint Council for Landscape Industries (1992). *Form of agreement for landscape works; supplementary memorandum, and Practice Note 3.* RIBA Publications Ltd, Finsbury Mission, 39 Moreland Street, London, EC1V 8BB.

Kerr, G. and Evans, J. (1993). *Growing broadleaves for timber.* Forestry Commission Handbook 9. HMSO, London.

MAFF (1981). *RB427: The analysis of agricultural materials.* HMSO, London.

Moffat, A. J. and Bending, N. A. D. (1992). *Physical site evaluation for community woodland establishment.* Research Information Note 216. Forestry Commission, Edinburgh.

Moffat, A. J. and McNeill, J. D. (1994). *Reclaiming disturbed land for forestry.* Forestry Commission Bulletin 110. HMSO, London.

Taylor, C. M. A. (1991). *Forest fertilisation in Britain.* Forestry Commission Bulletin 95. HMSO, London.

## Advice

Institute of Ecology and Environmental Management, 36 Kingfisher Court, Hambridge Rd, Newbury, Berkshire, RG14 5SJ.

Institute of Professional Soil Scientists, The Manor House, Castle Street, Spofforth, Harrogate, Yorkshire, HG3 1AR.

# 5 Establishing successful woodlands

Your specification and design will be of little value if they do not result in a successful woodland on the ground. Careful attention to the details of implementation can make the difference between success and failure.

## Ground preparation

Urban soils are often disturbed, compacted, infertile, drought prone, poorly drained or contaminated with toxic materials. The site assessment survey (Chapter 4, Site assessment) will determine the soil attributes needing amendment.

Amend soil physical conditions to:

- relieve compaction
- improve soil structure
- improve drainage
- remove or dilute rubble and stone.

Amend soil chemical conditions to:

- improve the supply of essential elements
- remove or dilute toxic substances.

### Dealing with compaction

The most common problem on urban planting sites is compaction and poor soil structure. Soil compaction reduces the retention and movement of air and water in the soil and can physically impede root penetration. Poor structure reduces soil moisture-holding capacity and so accentuates winter waterlogging and summer drought. You are likely to encounter three types of compaction.

- Compaction throughout the soil profile. Characteristic of land associated with industry and mineral workings where the ground has been compacted by heavy machinery.
- Compaction in the surface layers of the soil. Characteristic of amenity grassland or pasture land where superficial compaction results from pedestrian use, regular grass mowing and grazing animals.
- Plough pans. Compaction just below the depth of ploughing is common on ex-arable land, particularly with clay soils.

Plate 5.1 Compaction throughout a man-made soil profile showing phases in the site's history as an infilled open-cast coal mine, brick-works and coal storage area.

Plate 5.2 Wing-tined ripping on a 1.5 ha urban site in the West Midlands.

If trees are to thrive any compaction must be relieved before planting and this is best achieved when the soil is dry. Dry soil fractures and shatters well to give good soil disturbance. Soil disturbance is less when wet, and cultivation can cause smearing and loss of structure. There is only one opportunity to get ground preparation right – in the summer before planting. The specification and design must be ready in time to allow this.

Relieve compaction throughout the soil profile by deep cultivation, to 0.5 m on clay sites, and 0.7 m on sandy sites, using a wing-tine ripper. Tines should be spaced no wider than 1.2 m apart, with the outer ones positioned in line with the tractor tracks. Cross ripping perpendicular to the first pass is not usually required. On sites where buried rocks or other large debris are expected, conventional deep tines should be used. If the degree of cultivation is still not adequate, wing-tine ripping should then be undertaken, making sure that large boulders and pieces of debris are removed or clearly marked. After ripping, heavy discs are sometimes used as a final treatment to break up particularly large clods or to incorporate sewage sludge into the soil.

On small urban forestry sites wing-tine ripping using a purpose built implement may be impractical because of limited manoeuvrability and expensive because of high delivery charges. On several sites in the Midlands a much smaller and cheaper ripper has been successfully used (Plate 5.2); its conventional tines have had wings welded to their removable tips. Heavy duty agricultural subsoilers and power harrows have also been used successfully on some sites. However, with these smaller machines the soil surface and vegetation must be totally dry to achieve the best possible traction.

Compaction in the surface layers of the soil reduces moisture availability around the root system of the newly planted tree and reduces water and air movement into the soil. Relieve surface compaction using an agricultural chisel plough. Surface compaction can reform quickly after cultivation so, as with all types of ground preparation, avoid traffic over the cultivated soil, particularly when the ground is wet.

Even though plough pans do not normally affect the production of shallow-rooting annual arable crops, they do restrict the depth of tree rooting, making trees vulnerable to spring waterlogging, summer drought and instability. Agricultural subsoilers are designed to break up plough pans and are readily available at low cost through agricultural contractors or local farmers. Soils formed from swelling clays (for example Oxford clay and London clay) are prone to shrinkage in the summer and can crack badly down the rip lines. On these soils the planting position must be offset from the rip line to avoid exposing the tree roots to drying.

## Other forms of site amendment

Conventional restoration practice relies on the use of earthscrapers to replace soil-forming materials, which inevitably causes compaction. Restoration using the dump truck and backactor method can prevent compaction in the first place. Dump trucks tip the soil-forming material in heaps on the (if necessary, ripped) surface of the overburden and the soil is spread using a backactor with a wide bucket. At no stage is soil trafficked by earth-moving machinery and compaction can be almost entirely avoided.

On flat, low-lying sites that are prone to waterlogging, plant trees on ridges or mounds above the waterlogged zone. Hibberd (1991) gives details of forestry scarifiers and mounders designed to undertake this type of ground preparation but the location and small size of most urban forestry sites will mean that a backactor is usually the only viable option. A system of open drains may be needed to take excess water off the site.

Pit planting is expensive and on compacted sites results in trees that are slow growing, unstable, and prone to drought and waterlogging for many years. Consider it as a last resort for steep banks or very small areas where other cultivation equipment cannot be used. Planting pits should be at least $0.3 \times 0.3 \times 0.3$ m for forestry-type planting stock.

Research has found that the incorporation of organic amendments into planting pits is rarely beneficial and can be harmful. Organic amendments with high nutrient levels can reduce tree survival and growth because the resulting high soil-conductivity damages tree roots (products used at 30% volume/volume in the planting pit should have conductivities no higher than 4000 $\mu S$ per cm). Organic amendments make planting pit soil more coarsely textured than the surrounding soil. This can result in waterlogging in the winter and increased drought stress in the summer.

Water retentive polymers are sometimes prescribed for use in planting pits to reduce drought stress during the establishment phase. However, in field experiments these products have not increased the survival and growth of newly planted trees. This is because summer rainfall in lowland Britain is rarely heavy or prolonged enough to fully recharge the polymer once it has given up its water. Where irrigation is planned, water retentive polymers may allow an extension of the interval between irrigation treatments.

## Dealing with persistent soil problems

If the presence of toxic, inert or alkaline materials is beyond recommended limits (Chapter 4, Site assess-

ment) site reclamation may be needed and you should consult a reclamation engineer. Moffat and McNeill (1994) give more information on the reclamation of derelict sites.

Low fertility can be corrected using artificial fertilisers or sewage sludge, although repeated applications may be necessary. Some spoils, particularly colliery spoil, can be extremely acidic, requiring lime applications of up to 40 tonnes per ha before tree planting can be contemplated. In all cases, species must be selected which can tolerate the conditions inherent in the site. On particularly infertile sites species which can fix atmospheric nitrogen (such as the alders) increase the robustness of the planting mixture.

If small areas of soil within a site are affected by toxic or inert materials, these may need to be removed or covered with better quality soil-forming materials. However, if the soil problem is predominantly physical in nature, such as areas of pure sand or brick rubble, or due to chemical conditions not covered by the ICRCL safety thresholds, such as acidity, alkalinity or salinity, (Chapter 4, Site assessment) these areas are best left as open space in the woodland design.

## Fertiliser

The need for fertiliser should be determined before planting (Chapter 4, Site assessment). Nitrogen (N) is in short supply on most degraded urban sites and applications through the establishment phase will usually increase growth rates and improve the appearance of the trees. Phosphorus (P) is also often in short supply, but potassium (K) levels are usually adequate. Deficiency symptoms in the newly planted trees will indicate the potential benefit of further fertiliser applications during the

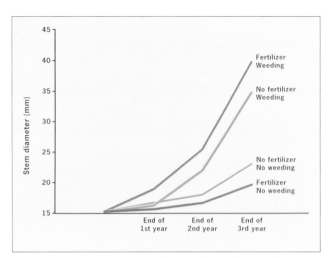

Figure 5.1 The effect of fertiliser and weed control on the growth of oak transplants.

**Table 5.1 Typical sewage sludge nitrogen (N) and phosphorus (P) analysis (from Wolstenholme _et al._ 1992)**

| Sludge type | Total | | Available[1] | |
|---|---|---|---|---|
| | **N** | **P** | **N** | **P** |
| Liquid digested (kg per m$^3$) | 1.8 | 0.6 | 0.6 | 0.3 |
| Liquid digested (kg per m$^3$) | 2.0 | 0.7 | 1.2 | 0.3 |
| Undigested cake (kg per tonne)[2] | 7.5 | 2.8 | 1.5 | 1.4 |
| Digested cake (kg per tonne) | 7.5 | 3.9 | 1.1 | 1.9 |

1  Available in the first growing season.
2  Wet tonnes.

establishment phase. Lime-induced chlorosis is a result of excessive soil alkalinity and shows as a yellowing of foliage. It is not easily corrected but careful species choice can minimise its incidence on high pH soils.

Whatever fertiliser is applied, it must be accompanied by weed control around the trees (Figure 5.1). Fertiliser application without weed control can actually reduce tree survival and growth. Because weeds are aggressive competitors they benefit from fertiliser application more than the establishing trees; the invigorated weeds then compete with the trees all the more aggressively for soil moisture.

## Sewage sludge

Composted wastes and animal manures are suitable forms of organic fertiliser but they are not usually available in the quantities required for urban woodlands. However, sewage sludge is a good source of nitrogen and phosphorus (Table 5.1) and should be considered as a fertiliser for urban forestry schemes.

Sewage sludge may be liquid or dewatered (cake), digested or undigested. Anaerobic digestion in heated tanks results in a more innocuous product with less odour and a lower pathogen content. Some water companies are now producing dry and pasteurised sludge products which are easy and totally safe to handle. It is the responsibility of the sludge supplier to analyse both sludge and soil for heavy metal content to ensure that ICRCL thresholds are not exceeded (Chapter 4, Site assessment).

Whilst sewage sludge can be expensive to spread, increasing pressure to find acceptable means of disposal is encouraging water companies to bear much of this cost. On impoverished sites, up to 100 m$^3$ per hectare of caked sludge or 400 m$^3$ per hectare of liquid sludge (in doses no greater than 100 m$^3$ per hectare to avoid run-off) can be applied before ground preparation. However, the resulting vigorous growth of vegetation between the weeded spots can swamp the trees and may require mowing. Similarly, open space will also require more frequent mowing unless application can be avoided on these areas.

Unpasteurised sewage sludge can contain pathogenic bacteria and viruses. Whilst the risk of infection is very low, current advice is to restrict public access for three months after surface application. This will rule out the use of some sewage sludges on urban sites. Wolstenholme *et al.* (1992) detail health and safety considerations of sewage sludge application.

---

**Deficiency symptoms on fully developed leaves in full light (from Taylor, 1991)**

**Nitrogen:** yellowing of the whole crown, reduced leaf size, leaves uniformly discoloured.

**Phosphorus:** stunted, dull green leaves. Purple or red tints at leaf margin in severe cases.

**Potassium:** yellowing of leaves, sometimes between veins, with marginal scorch in severe cases. Leaves inside crown may be less affected.

**Magnesium:** slight yellowing of leaves, especially between the veins where dead patches may develop in severe cases.

**Iron and manganese:** yellowing between leaf veins, similar to magnesium deficiency. Usually associated with lime-induced chlorosis, when iron and manganese become insoluble due to high pH.

---

### Artificial fertilisers

Artificial fertilisers vary in their formulation and release rate. Correct specific deficiencies using single element fertilisers and deficiencies of several elements with compound fertiliser of the appropriate formulation. Slow release fertilisers are most expensive but should be used where repeat doses cannot be applied.

Consider tractor application of P over the whole site before planting as this is quick and cheap. When soil pH is near neutral, soluble sources of P such as triple-superphosphate should be used – rock phosphate can become immobile.

Apply N as urea or ammonium nitrate at the start of the second growing season, by which time establishing trees will have a system of fine roots able to absorb it. Because N is not held in the soil, new planting may benefit from further applications during the establishment phase. Restrict N application to the weed-free $1.0 \times 1.0$ m around the tree. This minimises cost and avoids fertilising inter-row vegetation which tends to reduce sward diversity and may result in the need for mowing. Apply N only to those species that cannot fix it (i.e. not to alders and legumes). This avoids damaging the N-fixing capability of these species, minimises the cost of application, and gives a growth boost to the slower growing species. The use of N-fixing trees in intimate mixture with other species to provide a nutritional benefit is problematic and not usually practical (Chapter 5, Species mixtures).

## Species choice

There are two main considerations when choosing species for urban woodlands.

- Which species are suited to the site conditions?

63

- Of these species, which are suited to the objectives of the woodland?

Whatever the objectives of a scheme, the species used must be suited to the site. If species are chosen for purely aesthetic, commercial or objective-related reasons, either the scheme will fail to realise its objectives or considerable expense will be required to bring the site up to a standard sufficient to support the chosen trees. Evans (1984) and Anderson (1961) give practical advice on species selection on the basis of site type and vegetation.

Fertile sites with deep soils present few limitations to species choice. However, most urban sites are less hospitable and Tables 5.2 to 5.5 list species suitable for particular site conditions. If sites display more than one of the attributes covered by the tables (for example, a site that is drought prone and alkaline), suitable species will be present in both tables.

Having established a short-list of species suited to the site, the final choice will depend on the objectives of the scheme. On sites not radically altered by human activities, soil characteristics, vestiges of semi-natural vegetation, and tree species present in nearby woodlands and hedgerows may be used to indicate the species that are most appropriate for the site. On degraded sites choice is restricted to tolerant, often introduced, species which, if laid out and managed sensitively, can still create valuable naturalistic multi-purpose woodland. Urban planting schemes provide good opportunities for the imaginative use of species that may be inappropriate in rural areas. These species, as well as being tolerant of difficult site conditions, can add interest to a woodland through the variety of colour and form, and can provide wood that is particularly suited for use by local communities.

**Table 5.2  Species tolerant of dry sites**

|  | Species | Acidic | Alkaline |
|---|---|---|---|
| # | Field maple (Acer campestre) | | ✔* |
| * | Box elder (Acer negundo) | ✔* | ✔* |
| | Norway maple (Acer platanoides) | ✔ | ✔* |
| | Sycamore (Acer pseudoplatanus) | ✔* | ✔* |
| * | Silver maple (Acer saccharinum) | ✔* | ✔ |
| * | Tree of heaven (Ailanthus altissima) | ✔ | ✔* |
| * | Italian alder (Alnus cordata) | | ✔* |
| | Grey alder (Alnus incana) | ✔* | ✔ |
| | Caucasian alder (Alnus subcordata) | ✔* | |
| # | Silver birch (Betula pendula) | ✔ | ✔ |
| | Sweet chestnut (Castanea sativa) | | |
| # | Dogwood (Cornus sanguinea) | | ✔* |
| # | Hazel (Corylus avellana) | ✔ | ✔ |
| * | Turkish hazel (Corylus colurna) | ✔ | ✔* |
| * | Snow gum (Eucalyptus pauciflora sub. niphophila) | ✔ | |
| # | Beech (Fagus sylvatica) | | ✔ |
| * | Green ash (Fraxinus pennsylvanica) | ✔* | ✔* |
| | Maidenhair tree (Ginkgo biloba) | | ✔ |
| * | Honey locust (Gleditsia triacanthos) | ✔ | ✔* |
| *# | Sea buckthorn (Hippophae rhamnoides) | | ✔* |
| # | Holly (Ilex aquifolium) | ✔ | ✔* |
| # | Crab apple (Malus sylvestris) | ✔ | ✔ |
| * | White mulberry (Morus alba) | ✔ | ✔ |
| | London plane (Platanus acerifolia) | ✔ | ✔ |
| * | White poplar (Populus alba) | ✔* | ✔ |
| *# | Grey poplar (Populus canescens) | ✔* | ✔* |
| # | Wild cherry (Prunus avium) | | ✔ |
| # | Bird cherry (Prunus padus) | | ✔ |
| | Pear (Pyrus communis) | ✔ | ✔ |
| | Holm oak (Quercus ilex) | | ✔* |
| *# | Sessile oak (Quercus petraea) | ✔* | |
| # | English oak (Quercus robur) | ✔* | ✔* |
| * | Red oak (Quercus rubra) | ✔* | |
| *# | Purging buckthorn (Rhamnus cathartica) | | ✔* |
| * | False acacia (Robinia pseudoacacia) | ✔* | ✔* |
| * | Violet willow (Salix daphnoides) | | |
| *# | Whitebeam (Sorbus aria) | | ✔* |
| # | Rowan (Sorbus aucuparia) | ✔* | ✔ |

## Table 5.2  cont.

| | Acidic | Alkaline |
|---|---|---|
| # Small-leaved lime (Tilia cordata) | | ✔ |
| # Broad-leaved lime (Tilia platyphyllos) | | |
| *# Wayfaring tree (Viburnum lantana) | | ✔* |
| | | |
| * Algerian fir (Abies numidica) | | |
| * Atlas cedar (Cedrus atlantica) | | ✔ |
| Lawson cypress (Chamaecyparis lawsoniana) | ✔ | ✔ |
| * Leyland cypress (× Cupressocyparis leylandii 'Leighton Green') | ✔* | ✔ |
| * Smooth Arizona cypress (Cupressus glabra) | | |
| *# Common juniper (Juniperus communis) | ✔ | ✔* |
| * Oriental spruce (Picea orientalis) | ✔* | |
| * Corsican pine (Pinus nigra var. maritima) | ✔* | ✔* |
| *# Scots pine (Pinus sylvestris) | ✔ | ✔ |
| # Yew (Taxus baccata) | ✔ | ✔* |
| * Western red cedar (Thuja plicata) | ✔ | ✔* |
| Western hemlock (Tsuga heterophylla) | ✔* | |

Notes: Table 5.2
# Native to at least part of Great Britain (see Soutar and Peterken (1989) for geographical distributions).
* Particularly tolerant of the conditions indicated.

## Table 5.3  Species tolerant of wet sites

| | Acidic | Alkaline |
|---|---|---|
| # Field maple (Acer campestre) | | ✔* |
| * Box elder (Acer negundo) | ✔* | ✔* |
| Norway maple (Acer platanoides) | ✔ | ✔* |
| Sycamore (Acer pseudoplatanus) | ✔* | ✔* |
| * Red maple (Acer rubrum) | | |
| * Silver maple (Acer saccharinum) | ✔* | ✔ |
| * Italian alder (Alnus cordata) | | ✔* |
| *# Common alder (Alnus glutinosa) | ✔ | ✔ |
| * Grey alder (Alnus incana) | ✔* | ✔ |
| * Red alder (Alnus rubra) | ✔* | |
| * Caucasian alder (Alnus subcordata) | ✔* | |

## Table 5.3  cont.

| | Acidic | Alkaline |
|---|---|---|
| *# White birch (Betula pubescens) | | ✔ |
| # Hornbeam (Carpinus betulus) | | ✔ |
| Bitternut (Carya cordiformis) | | |
| # Hazel (Corylus avellana) | ✔ | ✔ |
| Turkish hazel (Corylus colurna) | ✔ | ✔* |
| # Common hawthorn (Crataegus monogyna) | ✔ | ✔ |
| *# Alder buckthorn (Frangula alnus) | | |
| * Green ash (Fraxinus pennsylvanica) | ✔* | ✔* |
| Maidenhair tree (Ginkgo biloba) | | ✔ |
| # Holly (Ilex aquifolium) | ✔ | ✔* |
| * Sweetgum (Liquidambar styraciflua) | | |
| # Crab apple (Malus sylvestris) | ✔ | ✔ |
| * White mulberry (Morus alba) | ✔ | ✔* |
| London plane (Platanus acerifolia) | ✔ | ✔ |
| * White poplar (Populus alba) | ✔* | ✔ |
| * Hybrid black poplars (Populus × canadensis) | | ✔* |
| *# Grey poplar (Populus canescens) | ✔* | ✔* |
| *# Black poplar (Populus nigra var. betulifolia) | | ✔* |
| *# Aspen (Populus tremula) | ✔* | |
| * Western balsam poplar (Populus trichocarpa) and cultivars | | ✔* |
| # Bird cherry (Prunus padus) | | ✔ |
| Pear (Pyrus communis) | ✔ | ✔ |
| * Pin oak (Quercus palustris) | | |
| # English oak (Quercus robur) | ✔* | ✔* |
| False acacia (Robinia pseudoacacia) | ✔* | ✔* |
| *# White willow (Salix alba) | | ✔* |
| *# Goat willow (Salix caprea) | ✔ | ✔* |
| *# Grey sallow (Salix cinerea) | ✔ | ✔* |
| *# Crack willow (Salix fragilis) | | ✔* |
| *# Bay willow (Salix pentandra) | | ✔* |
| *# Common osier (Salix viminalis) | | ✔* |
| # Rowan (Sorbus aucuparia) | ✔* | ✔ |
| # Small-leaved lime (Tilia cordata) | | ✔ |
| # Broad-leaved lime (Tilia platyphyllos) | | |
| # Guelder rose (Viburnum opulus) | | ✔* |
| | | |
| Atlas cedar (Cedrus atlantica) | | ✔ |
| Lawson cypress (Chamaecyparis lawsoniana) | ✔ | ✔ |

### Table 5.3 cont.

| | Acidic | Alkaline |
|---|---|---|
| Leyland cypress (× Cupressocyparis leylandii 'Leighton Green') | ✔* | ✔ |
| Hybrid larch (Larix × eurolepis) | ✔ | |
| Dawn redwood (Metasequoia glyptostroboides) | | |
| Norway spruce (Picea abies) | ✔ | ✔ |
| * Sitka spruce (Picea sitchensis) | ✔* | |
| * Lodgepole pine (Pinus contorta) | ✔* | |
| Corsican pine (Pinus nigra var. maritima) | ✔* | ✔* |
| # Scots pine (Pinus sylvestris) | ✔ | ✔ |
| Coast redwood (Sequoia semperivens) | | |
| Swamp cypress (Taxodium distichum) | | |
| Western red cedar (Thuja plicata) | ✔ | ✔* |
| * Western hemlock (Tsuga heterophylla) | ✔* | |

Notes: Table 5.3
# Native to at least part of Great Britain (see Soutar and Peterken (1989) for geographical distributions).
* Particularly tolerant of the conditions indicated.

### Table 5.4   Species tolerant of acid sites

| | Dry | Wet |
|---|---|---|
| * Box elder (Acer negundo) | ✔* | ✔* |
| Norway maple (Acer platanoides) | ✔ | ✔ |
| * Sycamore (Acer pseudoplatanus) | ✔ | ✔ |
| * Silver maple (Acer saccharinum) | ✔* | ✔* |
| Tree of heaven (Ailanthus altissima) | ✔* | |
| # Common alder (Alnus glutinosa) | | ✔* |
| * Grey alder (Alnus incana) | ✔ | ✔* |
| * Red alder (Alnus rubra) | | ✔* |
| * Caucasian alder (Alnus subcordata) | ✔ | ✔* |
| # Silver birch (Betula pendula) | ✔ | |
| # White birch (Betula pubescens) | | ✔* |
| # Hazel (Corylus avellana) | ✔ | ✔ |
| Turkish hazel (Corylus colurna) | ✔* | ✔ |
| # Common hawthorn (Crataegus monogyna) | | ✔ |
| Snow gum (Eucalyptus pauciflora sub. niphophila) | ✔* | |
| * Green ash (Fraxinus pennsylvanica) | ✔* | ✔* |
| Honey locust (Gleditsia triacanthos) | ✔* | |
| # Holly (Ilex aquifolium) | ✔ | ✔ |
| # Crab apple (Malus sylvestris) | ✔ | ✔ |
| White mulberry (Morus alba) | ✔* | ✔* |
| London plane (Platanus acerifolia) | ✔ | ✔ |
| *# White poplar (Populus alba) | ✔* | ✔* |
| *# Grey poplar (Populus canescens) | ✔* | ✔* |
| *# Aspen (Populus tremula) | | ✔* |
| Pear (Pyrus communis) | ✔ | ✔ |
| *# Sessile oak (Quercus petraea) | ✔* | |
| *# English oak (Quercus robur) | ✔* | ✔* |
| * Red oak (Quercus rubra) | ✔ | |
| * False acacia (Robinia pseudoacacia) | ✔* | ✔ |
| Goat willow (Salix caprea) | | ✔* |
| Grey sallow (Salix cinerea) | | ✔ * |
| *# Rowan (Sorbus aucuparia) | ✔ | ✔ |
| Lawson cypress (Chamaecyparis lawsoniana) | ✔ | ✔* |
| * Leyland cypress (× Cupressocyparis leylandii 'Leighton Green') | ✔* | ✔* |
| # Common juniper (Juniperus communis) | ✔* | |
| Hybrid larch (Larix × eurolepis) | | ✔ |
| Norway spruce (Picea abies) | | ✔ |
| * Oriental spruce (Picea orientalis) | ✔* | |
| * Sitka spruce (Picea sitchensis) | | ✔* |
| * Lodgepole pine (Pinus contorta var. contorta) | | ✔* |
| * Corsican pine (Pinus nigra var. maritima) | ✔* | ✔* |
| # Scots pine (Pinus sylvestris) | ✔* | ✔ |
| # Yew (Taxus baccata) | ✔ | |
| Western red cedar (Thuja plicata) | ✔* | ✔ |
| * Western hemlock (Tsuga heterophylla) | ✔ | ✔* |

Notes: Table 5.4
# Native to at least part of Great Britain (see Soutar and Peterken (1989) for geographical distributions).
* Will tolerate particularly acidic conditions (pH 3.5–4.5).

# Table 5.5  Species tolerant of alkaline sites

| | Species | Dry | Wet |
|---|---|---|---|
| *# | Field maple (Acer campestre) | ✔ | ✔ |
| * | Box elder (Acer negundo) | ✔* | ✔* |
| * | Norway maple (Acer platanoides) | ✔ | ✔ |
| * | Sycamore (Acer pseudoplatanus) | ✔ | ✔ |
| | Silver maple (Acer saccharinum) | ✔* | ✔* |
| * | Tree of heaven (Ailanthus altissima) | ✔* | |
| * | Italian alder (Alnus cordata) | ✔* | |
| # | Common alder (Alnus glutinosa) | | ✔* |
| | Grey alder (Alnus incana) | ✔ | ✔* |
| # | Silver birch (Betula pendula) | ✔ | |
| *# | Box (Buxus sempervirens) | | |
| # | Hornbeam (Carpinus betulus) | | ✔ |
| *# | Dogwood (Cornus sanguinea) | ✔ | |
| # | Hazel (Corylus avellana) | ✔ | ✔ |
| | Turkish hazel (Corylus colurna) | ✔* | ✔ |
| # | Hawthorn (Crataegus monogyna) | | ✔ |
| # | Beech (Fagus sylvatica) | ✔ | |
| *# | European ash (Fraxinus excelsior) | | |
| * | Green ash (Fraxinus pennsylvanica) | ✔* | ✔* |
| | Maidenhair tree (Ginkgo biloba) | ✔ | ✔ |
| * | Honey locust (Gleditsia triacanthos) | ✔* | |
| *# | Sea buckthorn (Hippophae rhamnoides) | ✔* | |
| *# | Holly (Ilex aquifolium) | ✔ | ✔ |
| # | Crab apple (Malus sylvestris) | ✔ | ✔ |
| * | White mulberry (Morus alba) | ✔* | ✔* |
| | London plane (Platanus acerifolia) | ✔ | ✔ |
| | White poplar (Populus alba) | ✔* | ✔* |
| * | Hybrid black poplars (Populus × canadensis) | | ✔* |
| *# | Grey poplar (Populus canescens) | ✔* | ✔* |
| *# | Black poplar (Populus nigra var. betulifolia) | | ✔* |
| * | Western balsam poplar (Populus trichocarpa) and cultivars | | ✔* |
| # | Wild cherry (Prunus avium) | ✔ | |
| # | Bird cherry (Prunus padus) | ✔ | ✔ |
| # | Blackthorn (Prunus spinosa) | | |
| | Wild pear (Pyrus communis) | ✔ | ✔ |
| * | Holm oak (Quercus ilex) | ✔ | |
| *# | English oak (Quercus robur) | ✔* | ✔* |
| *# | Purging buckthorn (Rhamnus catharticus) | ✔* | |

# Table 5.5  cont.

| | Species | Dry | Wet |
|---|---|---|---|
| * | False acacia (Robinia pseudoacacia) | ✔* | ✔ |
| *# | White willow (Salix alba) | | ✔* |
| *# | Goat willow (Salix caprea) | | ✔* |
| *# | Grey sallow (Salix cinerea) | | ✔* |
| *# | Crack willow (Salix fragilis) | | ✔* |
| # | Bay willow (Salix pentandra) | | ✔* |
| # | Common osier (Salix viminalis) | | ✔* |
| *# | Whitebeam (Sorbus aria) | ✔* | |
| # | Rowan (Sorbus aucuparia) | ✔ | ✔ |
| # | Small-leafed lime (Tilia cordata) | ✔ | ✔ |
| *# | Wayfaring tree (Viburnum lantana) | ✔* | |
| | Grecian fir (Abies cephalonica) | | |
| | Atlas cedar (Cedrus atlantica) | ✔* | |
| | Lawson cypress (Chamaecyparis lawsoniana) | ✔ | ✔ |
| | Leyland cypress (× Cupressocyparis leylandii) | ✔* | ✔* |
| *# | Common juniper (Juniperus communis) | ✔ | |
| * | Corsican pine (Pinus nigra var. maritima) | ✔* | ✔* |
| # | Scots pine (Pinus sylvestris) | ✔* | ✔ |
| | Douglas fir (Pseudotsuga menziesii) | | |
| *# | Yew (Taxus baccata) | ✔ | |
| | Western red cedar (Thuja plicata) | ✔* | ✔ |

Notes: Table 5.5

\# Native to at least part of Great Britain (see Soutar and Peterken (1989) for geographical distributions).

\* Particularly tolerant of the conditions indicated. (NB. Sites with a pH above 8.5 should not be considered for woodland creation).

## Species mixtures

The use of carefully planned mixtures can:

- improve the success and speed of woodland establishment;
- increase the amenity value of woodland; and
- facilitate the growing and harvesting of utilisable timber.

Newly planted trees experience high levels of stress and this is exacerbated by poor site quality and exposure. Tolerant species can be used to 'nurse' the more sensitive preferred species, by improving the microclimate on the planting site and protecting the preferred species from exposure. In addition, N-fixing species have the potential to improve the availability of nitrogen to the preferred species. As well as benefiting preferred species, tolerant species act as a fall back should the preferred species fail (Chapter 4, Practical woodland design).

Tolerant nurse species used in mixtures should be removed once they have done their job. Failure to do this will affect the character of the developing woodland and preferred species may be suppressed. Traditionally, the nurse crop is progressively removed when it has drawn the preferred species into good quality straight stems and has reached a saleable size itself. In urban woodlands, where a return from the nurse species is not an imperative, the process of removing the nurse can start much earlier. If the preferred species have established well, coppicing or removal of nurse trees can start as early as year five (Chapter 7, Silvicultural management of recently established woodlands).

The species in a mixture designed to be part of the long-term character of the woodland must be compatible. Your design must ensure that vigorous species do not suppress slower growing species and that the species mixture has the potential to create the desired woodland structure.

## Intimate mixtures

Whilst diverse at the individual tree level, intimate mixtures tend to give a homogeneous effect at the site level (Figure 5.2) resulting in a monotonous experience for site users and a limited diversity of

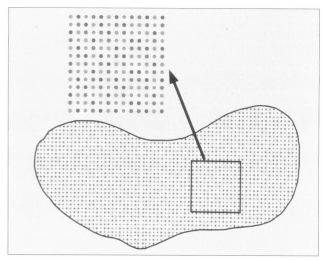

Figure 5.2 Intimate mixture of four species in equal proportion. At the compartment scale the impression is of a homogeneous woodland.

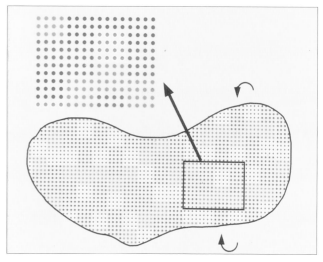

Figure 5.3 Regular mixture in square groups of 16 of four species in equal proportion (red, green, blue, yellow running top to bottom → bottom to top → etc., as would realistically be the case).

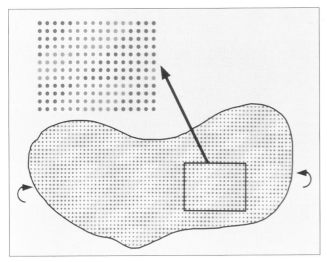

Figure 5.4 Regular mixture in staggered groups of 16 of four species in equal proportion (red, green, blue, yellow running left to right → right to left → etc., as would realistically be the case).

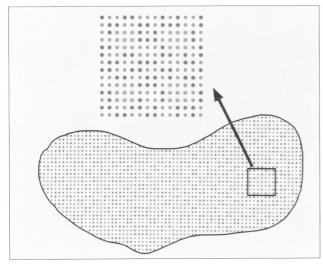

Figure 5.5 Final crop trees in groups of nine at final crop spacing within an intimately mixed matrix of 50% of one species and 25% each of another two species.

habitats for wildlife. In addition, the planting of complex intimate mixtures is expensive, and slower growing trees are likely to be suppressed by faster growing species. This presents a dilemma when nitrogen-fixing species are used to confer a nutritional benefit on preferred species. The nitrogen-fixing trees (alder, false acacia or laburnum) must be close enough to the recipient trees to confer a nutritional benefit but, before nitrogen becomes available through root and leaf decomposition, the vigorous nitrogen-fixing trees can out-grow and suppress the preferred species. The use of nitrogen-fixing shrubs (like green alder) may be a way around this problem.

## Group mixtures

Group mixtures (Figures 5.3 and 5.4) are more robust than intimate mixtures as the competition between slow and fast growing species is less, whilst the advantages of species diversity and nursing benefits remain. Group mixtures are more practical to plant than intimate mixtures as long as the species sequence is simple. Groups should generally be of between 9 and 25 trees, although understorey shrubs can be planted in smaller groups. A variant of group planting is to have a matrix of one species with (usually square) groups of 9 or 16 at the required final spacing for overstorey trees (about 100 groups per ha) (Figure 5.5). Management effort is focused on the groups which will form the mature woodland of the desired character.

## Random mixtures

Random mixtures are advocated for the creation of naturalistic woodlands. Species can be randomly planted in intimate mixture, but this has the disadvantages outlined above. More practical is to randomise the layout of single species groups

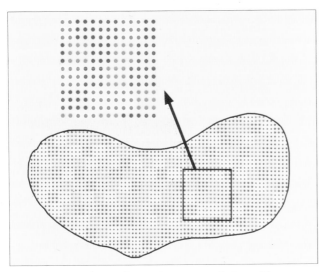

Figure 5.6 Random mixture in groups of nine of four species in equal proportion.

(Figure 5.6). Randomness is almost impossible to achieve unless some deliberate method is employed and the coloured bead technique is one approach. If a mixture of 65 % oak, 25 % birch and 10 % rowan is to be planted, 65 red beads (oak), 25 blue (birch) and 10 yellow (rowan) are placed in a pocket and each group of trees is planted according to the colour of the bead picked out of the pocket. Make sure that using random mixtures does not result in species being planted on a part of the site to which they are unsuited.

## Line mixtures

Line mixtures are a good way of organising a mixture to minimise the cost of management and maximise the return from thinning. Traditionally, the most favoured line mixture was three rows of conifers and three rows of broadleaves. At the time of first thinning the two outer rows of conifer are removed to create space for the broadleaves and yield an early economic return. About seven years later the centre row of conifer and the broadleaves are selectively thinned. After the third or fourth thinning the nurse crop is completely removed leaving pure broadleaved woodland. Because of their high landscape impact line mixtures are usually inappropriate where visually contrasting species are used (particularly mixtures of deciduous and evergreen) and where viewpoints look down onto the woodland.

## Single species

The use of only one species in a large compartment will not create the diversity that is usually beneficial for visual amenity and wildlife. However, there are circumstances where the simple splendour of a mature monoculture may offer an experience to site users that more complex mixtures cannot (Plate 5.3). Something of this effect may still be achieved by planting a single species overstorey with informal understorey planting over parts of the compartment (Figure 5.7).

In small woodlands (less than 3 ha) single overstorey species plots of 50 to 100 trees are often the most practical means of creating robust woodlands, particularly where differential growth rates between species may be a problem. Supplement this type of design with the planting of understorey species adjacent to the single species plots (Figure 5.8).

## How many species?

The number and proportion of species to use must be decided for the woodland as a whole and also for each part of the woodland which will need different proportions of species in relation to site characteristics and design criteria.

Plate 5.3 The simplicity that results from the use of a single species can be a great asset in some woodlands. (*29290*)

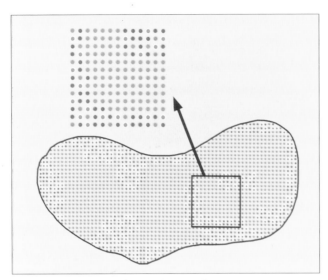

Figure 5.7 Compartment with a single overstorey species and three understorey species intimately mixed over parts of the site.

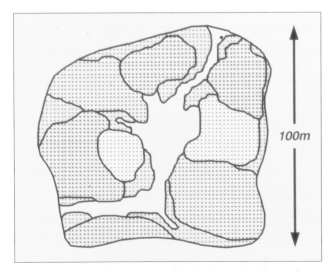

100m

Figure 5.8 A one hectare woodland planted with single species plots.

Many urban planting schemes contain more than 20 species resulting in a fussy, unnatural appearance as well as making the woodlands difficult to plant and manage. It is better to use the number of species that would occur in native woodland (see Rodwell and Patterson, 1994), which are predominantly composed of two or three dominant overstorey species and two or three frequently occurring understorey species. There may be three to six other tree species that occur infrequently. The distribution of species within native woodland is closely linked to spatial variation in topography and soil type. The Freckland Wood case study (Chapter 9, The final specification) illustrates the number and proportions of species used for the planting of a 20 ha colliery spoil mound.

## Planting-stock quality and type

The stresses experienced by trees planted onto degraded urban sites are severe and the best possible planting stock is needed to achieve success. The performance of planting stock is affected by its physical characteristics and its physiological condition. Physical characteristics are largely determined by the method of production in the nursery which results in stock types ranging from seedlings to semi-mature trees (Table 5.6; defined in British Standard 3936, Parts 1 and 4). Physiological condition is largely determined by the handling of the trees during transportation and planting, and prevailing site conditions in the year after planting.

### Bare-root trees

Bare-root trees are grown in outdoor nurseries to a variety of sizes. When ready for sale, the dormant trees are lifted and the soil is shaken from their

**Table 5.6   Stock types available for urban woodland planting**

| Stock type | | Usual height (cm) | Approximate cost* |
|---|---|---|---|
| **Bare-root** | | | |
| # | Seedling (1+0) | 15–30 | £0.14 |
| # | Transplant (1/2+1/2,1+1) | 20–120 | £0.16 |
| # | Undercut (1/2u1/2,1u1) | 30–60 | £0.16 |
| | Whip (1+2, 1+2+1, etc) | 120–180 | £1.00 |
| | Feathered to standard | 180–350 | £3.00+ |
| **Root-ball** | | | |
| | Half standards to semi-mature | 180+ | £10.00+ |
| **Container** | | | |
| # | Cell grown (seedling) | 15–30 | £0.18 |
| | Container grown (>1 year) | 50+ | £1.50 |
| | Containerised | 50+ | £1.50 |
| **Other** | | | |
| # | Cuttings | 20–30 | £0.20 |
| # | Sets | 70–200 | £1.40 |
| # | Seed | | £0.01 |

* For common species; 1993 prices.    # Suitable for urban woodland planting.

roots. The notations used in Table 5.6 are the recognised abbreviations for bare-root stock types. The numbers refer to years and '+' indicates when trees are transplanted into more spacious surroundings, usually from the crowded seed bed. The most commonly used type of forestry stock is the 1+1 (Plate 5.4) which has spent one year in the seed bed and one year in a transplant line. The 'u' indicates undercutting, when the lower parts of the root system are severed to promote a compact, well-branched and fibrous root system. Larger nurseries are increasingly turning to undercutting as a means of controlling root structure.

The predominant use of small bare-root stock in forestry is due, in part, to their low cost, but also to their better survival and growth rates. When large stock sizes are lifted from the nursery a high proportion of the root system is left behind. During the growing season the depleted root system is unable to supply the demands of the large crown and the tree dies back, remains slow growing and in poor condition for many years, or dies (Plate 5.5). The root system of small stock sizes is more complete when lifted from the nursery and hence more able to supply the lower water need of the smaller tree during the critical establishment phase.

Plate 5.5 Large planting stock often have inadequate root systems to supply the moisture needs of a large crown. The result is die-back or tree death. (*40969*)

Plate 5.4 A 1+1 transplant oak.

Plate 5.6 Plugs are cell-grown trees removed from the containers before despatch. (*40274*)

Whether transplants or undercuts are ordered, bare-root planting stock should have a fibrous, bushy root system. Although height is used most commonly to grade bare-root plants, the best indicator of suitability is the thickness of the root collar (where the root joins the shoot). Sturdy trees with a thick root collar are more likely to regenerate new roots quickly after planting. For a 30 cm tall bare-root plant a root collar diameter of at least 5 mm is desirable.

## Container trees

Containerised trees are bare-root trees that have been potted in the season before sale. This stock type is expensive and lacks the complete root system of container-grown stock so should not be used for urban woodland planting. Container-grown trees are raised in containers from seed and so have complete root systems. Because of their high cost they should be used for urban woodland planting only when a species, such as yew and holly, cannot be obtained as bare-root stock. Even in these situations the trees used should be less than 50 cm in height.

Cell-grown stock are produced in one growing season in low-volume containers and are suitable for urban woodland planting. There are two principal types of cell, the most common being reusable plastic containers from which the trees are removed for despatch as 'plugs' (Plate 5.6). Some nurseries still produce cell-grown stock in Japanese paper pots. With this system the trees are despatched in a biodegradable paper pot. Both of these container types ensure that trees are supplied with an intact root system.

Cell-grown stock is usually grown in polythene tunnels and needs a period of hardening off before despatch. Plants should be moved out of doors by late August, at which time fertilising should cease. Avoid cell-grown trees that are less than the British Standard 3936, Part 4 recommended 5 mm at the root collar for broadleaves and 3 mm for conifers.

Low-volume reusable plastic containers are good for local tree rearing schemes as they can be moved around and trees can be produced on a small scale (Chapter 3, Participation to benefit local people).

## Other stock types

Root-balled trees are grown outside in the nursery, usually to a large size. When lifted, a ball of soil is kept around the root system and wrapped in sacking. The cost of this stock type makes them unsuitable for urban woodland planting.

Cuttings and sets are commonly used for planting poplars and willows. Cuttings are most suitable for urban woodland planting and should be of one-year-old material from vigorous young trees (often coppiced annually to provide a supply of suitable material). Cuttings from the crowns of mature trees and from two-year-old wood should be avoided. Cuttings should be between 20 and 25 cm long with the top cut about 1 cm above a leaf bud and the bottom end close to or just below a bud. Sets are complete one-year-old shoots. They are more expensive than cuttings and used for planting at wide spacing in deep soils for the production of veneer quality timber. Sets are less susceptible than cuttings to mammal damage and physical swamping by weeds.

Direct seeding involves the sowing or planting of seed directly onto the woodland site (Chapter 6, Direct seeding).

**Plant handling**

**Steps to ensure that good quality stock is purchased and planted**

- Order plants in the summer before planting.
- If stock is available, buy locally to reduce transit time and facilitate nursery inspection.
- If possible, look at the plants in the nursery before buying. Good quality plants will be stout, of an even height, have high root to shoot ratios and have no visible defects.
- Order 5% above requirement to allow for on-site culling and other wastage.
- Ensure that trees are carefully and correctly packaged and transported. Bare-root trees and plugs should be transported in co-extruded black and white polythene bags. These bags are black on the inside to reduce the risk of frost damage to trees and white on the outside to reflect the sun's heat. The bags should be sealed.
- Minimise the amount of time that the trees are out of the ground. Tell the nursery when the plants are required so that they can lift the stock shortly before delivery. Plan work so that planting takes place soon after delivery.
- If the time of planting cannot be planned with certainty, cell-grown stock delivered in the containers can be kept throughout the planting season as long as they are watered and not exposed to frost. Stock delivered in sealed planting bags can be kept for up to 10 days in cool, shaded conditions. For longer periods stock must be temporarily heeled-in to ensure roots are kept moist.
- Plants must be handled carefully at all times.

Trees are living organisms and must be treated with care. The physiological condition of planting stock can be reduced by poor plant handling in four main ways.

- **Root drying.** Even on dull, cool days exposure to air can quickly desiccate roots.
- **Overheating.** If plants are stored or transported under a dark coloured tarpaulin, or in dark coloured or translucent polythene bags the temperatures experienced by the trees in sunny conditions can be damaging.
- **Frost damage.** The roots of lifted trees can be damaged or killed by freezing.
- **Physical damage.** Broken roots and shoots are visible but internal damage from rough handling also reduces the vigour of planting stock.

## Tree spacing

On the parts of the site where woodland is desired, sufficient trees must be planted to account for losses during the establishment phase. These losses can be particularly high on degraded urban sites where forestry stock should be planted at 4500 per ha (1.5 × 1.5 m spacing). Planting density can be reduced on better quality land but the need for rapid establishment of woodland cover on heavily used sites means that the minimum planting density around urban areas should usually be 2500 per ha (2.0 × 2.0 m spacing).

This is how you determine the required stocking density.

1. Decide what density of established trees is desired on the parts of the site to be wooded.

2. Estimate the likely level of survival during the establishment phase. On inhospitable sites and where pressure from site users is high, this

could be less than half, particularly if demanding species have been planted.

3. Divide the density of established trees required (1) by the proportion expected to survive (2). For example, 2000 established trees per ha are desired and 70% (0.7) survival is expected; the number of trees that should be planted is 2000 ÷ 0.7 = 2857.

The need to beat up may not be totally eliminated, but this approach does reduce reliance on beating up and minimises the duration of the vulnerable and management-intensive establishment phase.

## Planting

Whatever method of planting is used, an insistence on the highest quality of planting practice is always amply repaid in later years, and a high level of site supervision is essential once planting gets under way.

**Planting methods**

Notch planting (Figure 5.9) is appropriate on most sites. A garden spade can be used for making the notch, but a specially designed planting spade is more effective. On ripped sites there will be a choice of planting position. Where drought is likely to be a problem the tree should be planted about 15 cm from the rip line. On very wet sites the tree can be planted over the rip line and, if possible, on small mounds. If the ground to be planted is vegetated the notch can be cut into the sward and weed control applied later. Alternatively a square of turf can be can be cut out first and either removed, with the notch being cut directly into the exposed soil (screef planting), or inverted with the notch being cut through the turf (turf planting). Both of these

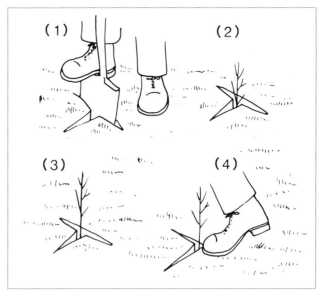

Figure 5.9 Planting transplants using the T-notch method.

methods give a measure of short-term weed control and may reduce the extent to which notches re-open in the summer.

Pit planting should not be used as an alternative to whole site ground preparation. However, there are situations where a small pit dug with a spade or mattock is the most appropriate method of planting on already cultivated sites:

• where planting stock has very bushy root systems and is difficult to notch plant; and

• where soils derived from swelling clays shrink during summer, opening up the planting notch and exposing tree roots to drying and contact with herbicides.

The method of planting cuttings is shown in Figure 5.10. Both cuttings and sets must be planted in well-cultivated ground to ensure good contact between the set and soil. On deep soils sets are

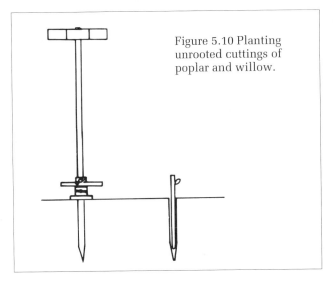

Figure 5.10 Planting unrooted cuttings of poplar and willow.

planted into holes to a depth of one-third the length of the set, but on poorer ground sets must be planted in deep planting pits.

## Time of planting

Trees should be planted whilst dormant. Planting any stock when it is actively growing will reduce establishment success because the root system of the stressed tree will not be able to provide the immediate water needs of the foliage. In the lowlands, stock is usually dormant from October to the end of March, although in mild autumns it may be into November before plants can be lifted in the nursery, and in mild springs flushing of some species can begin in mid March. Cell-grown stock can be despatched from the nursery at any time and may be planted from late September in years when late summer rainfall has been plentiful.

Trees should only be planted when site conditions are suitable, which can exclude much of January and February if soils are frozen or waterlogged. Beyond early April soils may already be too dry to provide the needs of trees that are already flushing. Some nurseries cold store trees to delay flushing, thus allowing later planting, but this is a viable option only on particularly wet sites.

So, the periods when both the trees and the site are suitable for planting are:

- late October (possibly late September for cell-grown stock) to the end of December: favoured on dry sites as some root growth may occur before soils get too cold, which prepares the tree to withstand spring drought;
- late February to the end of March: favoured on wet sites as trees do not have to suffer the ravages of a hard winter on a waterlogged planting site; however, if there is any risk of planting being held up it should be planned for the autumn rather than being pushed into April.

## Beating up

Beating up is the replacement of dead trees in the years after planting. There should be little need in robust woodlands, but if there are higher than expected losses the site should be brought back to the original stocking density at the end of the first and second growing seasons. If appropriate aftercare is undertaken, there should be no further need to beat up, stocking being sufficient to bear any further moderate losses without putting the creation of a woodland environment at risk. Beating up with fast growing species minimises the extension of the establishment maintenance phase.

Beating up provides a good opportunity for increasing the species diversity of new woodlands, particularly around the edge of compartments where the opportunity can be taken to strengthen the understorey, or to key compartments together by increasing the overlap of species.

The beat up requirement must be determined during the summer by counting the number of live plants in a series of 0.01 ha sample plots. On relatively homogeneous sites with few species, use 12 plots for schemes under 5 ha and 15 plots for larger schemes. Variable sites and complicated designs will require more plots for accurate assessment. Plots should be located systematically over the site. Try to determine the principal reasons for losses. This may indicate the need to use more tolerant species, to protect trees against damage, or to allow certain areas to revert to open space.

## Implementing the design plan

At planting, the design plan must be accurately translated into woodland on the ground. The importance of designing with implementation in mind to make this process straightforward has already been stressed (Chapter 4, Practical woodland design). The simpler the design the more likely that it will be laid out accurately. Because of the difference in species mix between compartments, it is usually best to advise planting one compartment at a time.

For very simple designs with a few, large compartments a careful briefing of operatives may be sufficient, particularly if the design plan contains reference points that are clearly visible on and around the site. For more complex or sensitive designs reference points can be provided. Draw a grid on the design plan, at a scale appropriate to the size and complexity of the site, and insert stakes on the site corresponding to the grid intersection points on the design plan.

For particularly complex or sensitive designs the 'pantomime horse method' can be used to mark the plot boundaries on the ground (Plate 5.7). One person holds the layout plan and walks the plot boundaries whilst the other follows directly behind marking the boundary with spray paint. Operatives then simply fill in the marked plots with the relevant species.

Plate 5.7  The 'pantomime horse' method of laying out complex new woodlands.

# Tree protection

Mammal damage to newly planted trees can be a serious problem, even in populated areas. Whilst deer numbers might be low close to towns, the potential for damage from voles, rabbits, hares and domesticated animals can be high. Damage during the vulnerable establishment phase extends the establishment period, reduces stocking and, in extreme cases, virtually destroys the woodland.

There are three options for control of mammal damage:

**Table 5.7   Height of tree protection required against different mammal pests (adapted from Kerr and Evans, 1993)**

| Animal | Individual tree protection | Fencing | Notes |
|---|---|---|---|
| Cattle and horses | Generally not viable | Standard stock fence (without barbed wire for horses) | A buffer zone is needed between stock fence and trees |
| Sheep | 1.8 m (if sheep are to have regular access, two tall stout stakes are needed) | Standard stock fence | |
| Deer: red, sika, fallow, roe, muntjac | 1.8 m<br>1.2 m | 2.0 m<br>1.8 m | |
| Hares | 0.75 m | 1.0 m. Use rabbit netting with a line wire 10 cm above the netting | |
| Rabbits | 0.6 m | 0.9 m. 15 cm at base turned away from the area to be protected and secured by turves | Landowners are legally required to control rabbits<br><br>Rabbits can be gassed from October to mid March |
| Voles | Vole guards 20 cm tall, buried at least 5 mm into the soil | Vole guards may be required in fenced areas if weed control is not meticulous | Good weed control will reduce the risk of damage<br><br>Treeshelters will not protect against voles unless staked firmly and buried 5 mm into the soil |

1. fencing (not effective against voles)
2. individual tree protection
3. controlling animal numbers.

Killing mammal pests is rarely practical or popular in urban situations, although land owners are legally obliged to control rabbits on their land if they are interfering with the use of neighbouring land (Chapter 2, Urban woodlands and the law). You will generally need to choose between fencing and individual tree protection (Table 5.7); the decision depending on:

- the size of the area to be planted
- the shape of the area to be planted
- planting density
- aesthetic considerations

- the desirability of freedom of movement and access
- the risk of vandalism.

The first three factors relate to the cost of protection. A calculation of relative costs should be made for each site to be planted (Table 5.8). Once the cost consequences of the decision on protection type are known, the other three factors must be considered. Some types of individual tree protection are visually obtrusive and can draw attention to the trees and attract vandalism. However, fencing restricts the movement of site users and can be stolen. Whichever protection method is used, regular inspection is obviously crucial.

Fencing heights for different mammal pests are given in Table 5.7. British Standard 1722: Part 2

**Table 5.8  Calculation for cost-effective tree protection against damage by mammals**

| | Animal pests | Site 1 | Site 2 |
|---|---|---|---|
| | | Roe deer and rabbits | Rabbits |
| **The planting site** | | | |
| Shape | | Rectangular | Triangular |
| Dimension | | 100 × 60 m | 200 × 400 × 450 m |
| Area | | 0.6 ha | 4 ha |
| Number of plants | | 1200 (2000 per ha) | 12000 (3000 per ha) |
| **Fencing** | | | |
| Fence length | | 320 m | 1050 m |
| Fence cost (per m) | | £4.10 (for deer fencing) | £2.40 (for rabbit fencing) |
| Total fencing cost | | **£1312** | **£2488** |
| **Individual tree protection** | | | |
| Cost of treeshelter | | £1.00 (for 1.2 m shelters) | £0.60 (for 0.6 m shelters) |
| Total treeshelter cost | | **£1200** | **£7200** |
| **Most economical protection** | | Treeshelters | Fencing |

## Treeshelter specification

**Size.** Height must be above the maximum browse level of the animal (see Table 5.7).

**Cross-sectional shape.** Square: can be flat packed for easy storage and transport, but can blow flat in strong winds. Round: less prone to wind distortion but bulky to store and transport even though differing diameters fit together in nests of three.

**Stake.** When erected the stake should be shorter than the treeshelter to avoid stem abrasion when the tree emerges from the shelter, and driven 30 cm into the ground. Stakes must be at least 25 × 25 mm in cross section.

**Ties.** Should be quick and easy to secure and release to allow inspection and maintenance.

**Lip.** The lip of the treeshelter should be folded or curved outwards, to avoid abrasion and breakage of soft leading shoots.

**Colour:** Colour should be chosen to blend in with the landscape, light brown and some shades of green being most commonly available. When planting under the shade of existing trees clear treeshelters should be used.

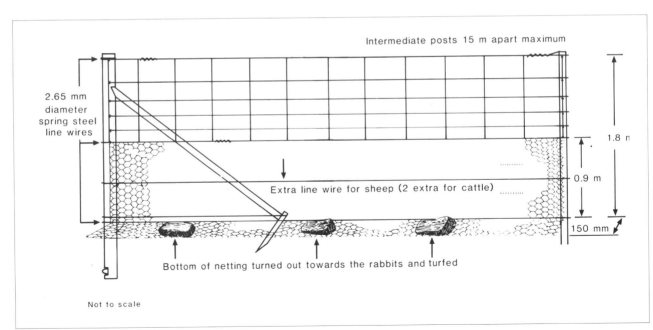

Figure 5.11 A deer and rabbit proof fence.

gives the specification for rectangular wire mesh (for deer and stock) and hexagonal wire netting (for rabbits and hares) (Figure 5.11), and fencing techniques are described in Pepper (1992). Consider the practicalities of fencing at the design stage. The line of a fence can greatly influence its cost as it affects fence length and the number of strainer posts used. Where possible, straight lengths for fencing should be maximised. This may mean enclosing some land to be left as open ground, or exclosing outlying groups of trees which can be individually protected.

Treeshelters are translucent polypropylene tubes which protect trees from mammal pests and provide a favourable microclimate around the tree by acting as a mini greenhouse. Their use is fully described in Potter (1991) which recommends that treeshelter height should principally reflect the mammal pests present (Table 5.7). As well as protection from damage, treeshelters accelerate early height growth, although diameter and root growth is not increased proportionally. Consequently, if treeshelters are removed prematurely the trees may be unable to support themselves. Treeshelters offer protection from herbicide damage and make trees easy to find in dense vegetation. However, in areas with high levels of public access, treeshelters can attract unwanted attention to the trees, and removal or damage of the shelter will leave the tree vulnerable to mammal damage.

Split plastic tubes protect tree stems from mammal and strimmer damage. For protection from voles (Plate 5.8) they should be 20 cm tall and pushed 5 mm into the soil. Taller split plastic tubes have been used to protect against rabbit damage but much forestry planting stock is neither tall nor sturdy enough to support them.

Spiral guards are loosely coiled plastic tubes which are used to reduce bark stripping by rabbits.

Plate 5.8 Severe vole damage has killed this two-year-old grey alder. Protection must be provided before damage gets this severe.

Plate 5.9 Reliance on individual tree protection can have a negative landscape impact during the establishment phase, is expensive with high density planting, and can attract unwanted attention to the trees. (*40962*)

They are only suitable for sturdy trees that are taller than the 60 cm height of protection needed, and that have sufficient side branches to hold the guard in place.

Plastic mesh guards are staked plastic netting tubes. They are generally only suitable for protecting the leading shoot of newly planted trees from rabbit damage, but for species with poor apical dominance even the leading shoot may grow through the netting, becoming vulnerable to damage from mammals and strangulation by the netting. Plastic netting is more commonly used to protect established trees from bark stripping by livestock.

## Weed control around trees

### The effect of weeds around trees

Weeds, particularly grasses, are fast growing and compete aggressively with newly planted trees for moisture and essential elements. Tall weeds compete with small trees for light causing new growth to be spindly and prone to physical damage. Rank weed growth can totally swamp small trees, reducing growth, or causing deformity or death. A cover of weeds provides an ideal habitat for voles which damage and kill trees. The result of competition with weeds is slow growth and death of trees.

If trees are already weak due to poor plant handling, or are planted onto impoverished sites with low moisture-holding capacity, the effect of weed competition can be virtually complete failure of the new woodland by the second growing season. Slow growing, moribund trees will remain vulnerable to other types of damage and stress for many years.

### Principles of weed control

Careful and well-timed weed control can have a dramatic effect on tree survival and growth (Plates 5.10 and 5.11) and is crucial to the success of any tree planting. Whatever method is used to kill weeds, trees must be freed from competition around their rooting zone until rooting is extensive and deep enough for the tree to compete with weeds. Trees will benefit from weed control over the whole rooting zone throughout their life (as is often undertaken in orchards) but this is not practical, cost effective or environmentally acceptable for woodland planting. The compromise is to keep 1 m² around each tree weed free, or to maintain a 1 m wide weed-free strip along the rows of trees. The provision of weed-free conditions is particularly important during the growing season, which starts

Plate 5.10 Three-year-old wild cherry without weed control. (*40203*)

in mid April and ends in September. There may be opportunities to control perennial weeds in the autumn before planting to ensure weed-free conditions at the start of the growing season.

On sites that will support rapid tree growth the duration of weed control should be three years, by which time tree root spread will be extensive. On difficult urban sites establishment will be slower and so weed control should be routinely continued for five years.

### Herbicides

Herbicides can be an effective and economical way of killing weeds. Herbicides approved for forestry are described in Willoughby and Dewar (1995). There are two broad groups of herbicides.

Plate 5.11 Three-year-old wild cherry with effective weed control. (*40199*)

Plate 5.12 Three-year-old wild cherry in regularly mown grass sward. (*40202*)

85

- Foliar acting herbicides are most commonly used for woodland establishment. They are absorbed at the point of contact on the leaf and the stem, and give best results when applied to actively growing weeds. Few foliar acting herbicides are highly selective and in most cases it is necessary to guard trees against spray contact, or use application methods which avoid contact with tree leaves.

- Residual herbicides act via the soil where they are taken up by weed roots. To be effective most must be applied to non-cloddy, damp soil and further rain is needed to wash them into the top 2 to 3 cm. Large soil clods will weather and crumble, exposing untreated soil and allowing weed growth. Because of these requirements residual herbicides are of most use for tree planting on cultivated arable land.

---

**Why you should kill weeds around newly planted trees**

- Eliminates competition for limited soil moisture.
- Maximises the amount of rainfall that percolates into the soil.
- Increases spring soil temperatures, promoting early tree root growth.
- Reduces competition for nutrients.
- Eventually contributes to the supply of nutrients as the dead weeds decompose.
- Reduces the shading and physical swamping effects of trees.
- Discourages voles from damaging trees.
- Reduces weed seed production from newly planted woodlands.

---

## Mulches

Mulches are materials that cover the ground and physically prevent weed growth.

- Organic mulches can control weeds effectively if applied, at considerable expense, over the whole of a previously weeded site. Applications around each tree may control weeds for one growing season but are rapidly invaded by weeds and need replacing at least annually. Consequently, organic mulches such as bark and wood chips are not cost effective for weed control in urban woodlands, but may usefully form part of a community participation programme.

- Sheet mulches can be applied individually around each tree or as a 1 m wide strip down rows of trees. Whilst more expensive than herbicides, sheet mulches can provide two or three years of weed control if durable materials are used and properly applied. However, do not consider sheet mulches as a one-visit tree-establishment system as they frequently become torn, tattered and displaced. Invigorated weed growth around the mat and through the hole for the tree stem can greatly reduce the area of effective weed control. If surrounded by rank grass, mulch mats can be colonised by voles which kill and damage trees.

## Other forms of weed control

Mowing keeps grass growing throughout the summer and so increases competition for soil moisture (Plate 5.12). Mowing or strimming of vegetation directly around trees often causes physical damage and tree losses and so should be considered only for the management of inter-row vegetation. If vegetation around newly planted trees has become rank some removal using hand tools may be required

# Herbicides or mulch mats?

## Herbicides

*Advantages*

Cost-effective.

Quick to apply.

Can be selective about which ground vegetation species are killed.

*Disadvantages*

Operatives must be trained and certificated so not suited to volunteers.

Needs a continuing commitment to aftercare.

Damage or death of trees can result from careless use.

Should be applied only when weather or soil conditions are right.

## Mulch mats

*Advantages*

Can give 2–3 years of weed control if a durable material is correctly applied.

Can be applied by volunteers.

Can recycle waste materials like old carpets and vinyl.

*Disadvantages*

More expensive than chemical weed control.

Poorly laid or poor quality material can lift and break up.

Must be regularly inspected.

Can invigorate weed growth around the mulch and through the hole for the tree stem.

Can look unsightly and attract unwanted attention to the trees.

Can harbour voles.

before herbicides can be applied, to minimise the risk of herbicide contact with the trees.

Cultivation can temporarily remove or check weeds and some forms of ground preparation can reduce weed competition in the first growing season. However, continued weed control by cultivation with hand tools is expensive and offers little satisfaction to volunteers as it must be repeated four or five times a season.

## Vegetation management between trees

Most of the land in newly planted woodlands is not occupied by trees. On the parts of the site that are planted, 75% of ground falls outside the weed-free spots with planting at $2.0 \times 2.0$ m and 56% at $1.5 \times 1.5$ m. Unplanted space must be managed according to the objectives of the woodland.

### Management of inter-row vegetation

On impoverished urban woodland sites inter-row vegetation is unlikely to swamp the newly planted trees and so should not need mowing. The low intensity of inter-row vegetation management is important to the informal appearance of urban woodlands and can result in attractive ground flora, particularly where grazing pressure has been relieved and where the sward is not dominated by coarse grasses. In addition, the opportunity is provided for woody colonisation to increase diversity and break up planting patterns. On exposed sites inter-row vegetation can provide valuable shelter to newly planted trees.

Cutting inter-row vegetation is expensive and can result in mechanical damage to the trees. It is warranted only when:

- inter-row vegetation is likely to swamp the establishing trees;
- the risk of fire is particularly high (mowing 5 m into the planted area along paths may be a cost-effective solution; Chapter 7, Protection of existing woodlands);
- the seeding of arable weeds is likely to cause a nuisance on neighbouring land; or
- increasing sward diversity is an important objective (Chapter 8, Woodlands for wildlife).

Using selective herbicides that kill only grasses on grass dominated sites can result in a dramatic increase in the range of flowering plants. Species-specific herbicides may be of value to eradicate particular problem species like thistle and docks.

A more intensive approach to managing inter-row vegetation is to sow the desired ground flora species into a cultivated seed bed. This is expensive and requires careful management but may be an attractive option in certain situations where the risk of tree losses is low and hence the plant spacing can be wide enough for tractor access.

- Low-productivity (usually fescue-based) grass swards can be sown on fertile arable land to prevent an explosion of arable weeds. The sward is most easily established in the spring or autumn before planting, but can be sown as strips between the rows of trees after planting.
- Low-productivity grass/wildflower mixtures can be sown on bare sites or where existing vegetation is uninteresting (Plate 5.13). Light-demanding species found in meadow mixes are most appropriate although many will eventually die out after canopy closure. True woodland plants are difficult to establish in full-light conditions due to competition from more aggressive species (Chapter 8, Woodlands for wildlife).

Plate 5.13  The sowing of wild flowers can add interest
to establishing woodland. (*40178*)

- Nitrogen-fixing legume species can be sown to increase nitrogen supply to the establishing trees. However, legume species such as clovers and vetches compete aggressively for moisture and will rapidly colonise the weed-free patch around each tree.
- Silvo-arable systems combine timber production with arable cropping. They require the planting of trees at very wide spacing and have only been undertaken on fertile arable land with fast growing poplars. Silvo-arable systems require intensive management and are more a method of maximising cropping potential than a means of creating woodland. Consequently such systems will rarely be appropriate in the urban environment.

## Management of open space

Open space may need regular cutting where access is to be encouraged. In large glades or rides differential mowing regimes can contribute to the development of woodland edge (Chapter 8, Woodlands for wildlife) and reduce mowing costs. On impoverished sites vegetation may not require mowing at all, treading by site users being enough to define paths, although ride mowing can be a useful tool for channelling site users. Take care not to lose the informal atmosphere of urban woodlands by over-zealous mowing regimes. The judicious use of selective herbicides can increase the floristic diversity and interest of open space.

# For more information

## Publications

Anderson, M. L. (1961). *The selection of tree species*. Oliver and Boyd, Edinburgh.

British Standards Institution (1984). *British Standard 3936 Part 4: Specification for forest trees.* BSI Standards, Milton Keynes.

British Standards Institution (1984). *British Standard 1722 Part 2: Specification for rectangular wire mesh and hexagonal wire netting fences.* BSI Standards, Milton Keynes.

British Standards Institution (1992). *British Standard 3936 Part 1: Specification for trees and shrubs.* BSI Standards, Milton Keynes.

The Committee for Plant Supply and Establishment (1985). *Plant handling.* The Horticultural Trades Association, 19 High Street, Theale, Reading, Berkshire, RG7 5AH. (01734) 303132.

Davies, R. J. (1987). *Trees and weeds.* Forestry Commission Handbook 2. HMSO, London.

Dobson, M. C. and Moffat, A. J. (1993). *The potential for woodland establishment on landfill sites.* HMSO, London.

Evans, J. (1984). *Silviculture of broadleaved woodland.* Forestry Commission Bulletin 62. HMSO, London.

Hibberd, B. G. (ed.) (1991). *Forestry practice.* Forestry Commission Handbook 6. HMSO, London.

Hodge, S. J. (1991). *Cell-grown broadleaved stock.* Arboriculture Research Note 98/91/ARB. Arboricultural Advisory and Information Service, Alice Holt Lodge, Farnham, Surrey GU10 4LH.

Hodge, S. J. (1991). *Amenity tree planting with bare-root stock.* Arboriculture Research Note 97/91/ARB.

Arboricultural Advisory and Information Service, Alice Holt Lodge, Farnham, Surrey GU10 4LH.

Hodge, S. J. (1993). *Trials of organic backfill amendments on trunk road sites.* Arboriculture Research Note 114/93/ARB. Arboricultural Advisory and Information Service, Alice Holt Lodge, Farnham, Surrey GU10 4LH.

Jobling, J. (1990). *Poplars for wood production and amenity.* Forestry Commission Bulletin 92. HMSO, London.

Kerr, G. and Evans, J. (1993). *Growing broadleaves for timber.* Forestry Commission Handbook 9. HMSO, London.

Moffat, A. J. and McNeill, J. D. (1994). *Reclaiming disturbed land for forestry.* Forestry Commission Bulletin 110. HMSO, London.

Pepper, H. W. (1992). *Forest fencing.* Forestry Commission Bulletin 102. HMSO, London.

Potter, M. J. (1991). *Treeshelters.* Forestry Commission Handbook 7. HMSO, London.

Rodwell, J. and Patterson, G. (1994). *Creating new native woodlands.* Forestry Commission Bulletin 112. HMSO, London.

Soutar, R. G. and Peterken, G. F. (1989). Regional lists of native trees and shrubs for use in afforestation schemes. *Arboricultural Journal,* **13 (1)**, 33–43.

Taylor, C. M. A. (1991). *Forest fertilisation in Britain.* Forestry Commission Bulletin 95. HMSO, London.

White, J. E. J. and Patch, D. (1990). *Propagation of lowland willows by winter cuttings.* Arboriculture Research Note 85/90/SILS. Arboricultural Advisory and Information Service, Alice Holt Lodge, Farnham, Surrey GU10 4LH.

Williamson, D. R. (1992). *Establishing farm woodlands.* Forestry Commission Handbook 8. HMSO, London.

Willoughby, I. and Dewar, J. (1995). *The use of herbicides in the forest.* Forestry Commission Field Book 8. HMSO, London.

Wolstenholme, R., Dutch, J., Moffat, A. J., Bayes, C. D. and Taylor, C. M. A. (1992). *A manual of good practice for the use of sewage sludge in forestry.* Forestry Commission Bulletin 107. HMSO, London.

# 6  Woodland creation from seed

Tree planting will usually be the most reliable method of woodland creation, especially where particular species and proportions of species are required. However, sowing seed directly onto the site or allowing the site to colonise naturally are options for woodland establishment which may offer benefits under some circumstances.

## Natural colonisation

Natural colonisation is the process of woodland creation on previously unwooded sites by natural seed dispersal. Whilst it offers a naturalistic vegetation structure and distribution (Plate 6.1), the manager has very little control over the speed of the process and the character of the woodland that develops.

Woodland creation by natural colonisation can be a very slow process. In a Forestry Commission Research Division survey of 47 abandoned urban and urban edge sites, only 20 % of quadrats examined were sufficiently colonised for woodland creation within 10 years of abandonment. This figure remained more or less constant until sites had been abandoned for more than 35 years.

For woody colonisation to occur at all there must be a suitable seed supply and it follows that species with poor powers of dispersal are least likely to colonise urban sites. The survey found the frequency of colonisation of most species to be closely linked to the presence of parent trees. The degree of urbanisation appeared to influence the amount of colonisation from both bird-dispersed seed and the heavier windblown seeds such as ash and sycamore (Table 6.1). Disturbance of birds and lack of suitable habitat reduces numbers of berry eating birds in urban areas and the generally sparse tree cover reduces the dispersal opportunities for the heavier windblown seeds. However, even given an adequate seed supply, conditions on the site must be conducive to germination and establishment.

**Table 6.1  Proportions of seed types by intensity of urbanisation from a Forestry Commission Research Division survey of abandoned urban sites**

|  | Light windblown seed | Heavy windblown seed | Bird - dispersed seed |
|---|---|---|---|
| Avon (lightly urbanised) | 1% | 40% | 56% |
| South Staffordshire (moderately urbanised) | 56% | 26% | 16% |
| West Midlands (intensely urbanised) | 91% | 1% | 7% |

Plate 6.1  Naturally colonised woodland on coal spoil
heaps abandoned in 1910.

Figure 6.1 The effect of vegetation type on colonisation to a woodland standard from a Forestry Commission Research Division survey of abandoned urban sites.

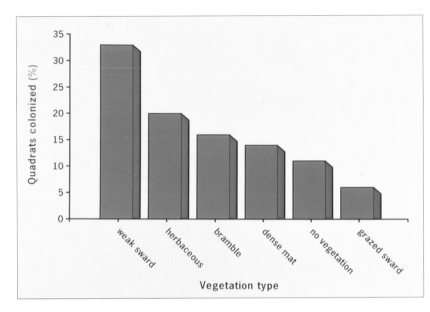

Plate 6.2 The rank grass on the more fertile soil in the background has prevented colonisation, but birch and sallow colonisation is prolific on the poorer area in the foreground. (*40979*)

In the absence of ground vegetation, fertile, moist sites will be colonised most quickly and by the widest range of species. However, these sites are also most favourable to rank ground vegetation. Rapid invasion of coarse grasses and other vegetation prevents seed from making contact with the mineral soil and competes for moisture and light with seed that does germinate (Figure 6.1). In contrast, on the most impoverished sites little ground vegetation develops but moisture and nutrient stress are so great that woody colonisation cannot establish either. Woody colonisation is most likely on sites that are sufficiently infertile and moisture stressed to prevent the rapid dominance of rank vegetation (weak sward in Figure 6.1), but not so stressed as to prevent the establishment of woody seedlings (no vegetation in Figure 6.1; Plate 6.2).

Woodlands formed by natural colonisation are generally species poor; the survey recorded an average of three species per site. The most common species recorded were ash, birch, goat willow, hawthorn, blackthorn and oak, although the species most likely to colonise and the species diversity varied between the three survey locations (Figure 6.2). In the relatively rural hinterland of Bristol (Avon) 17 species were recorded; in moderately urbanised south Staffordshire 13 species and in the heavily urbanised West Midlands 11 species were recorded. Species numbers were undoubtedly limited by reduced seed dispersal in the more urban situations, but the predominant site types also varied between locations and this influenced the species composition of colonisation.

Goat willow and birch were most prevalent on infertile sites supporting a weak sward; hawthorn was more common on densely vegetated, fertile sites. Ash was most prevalent on subsoil where fertility was moderate but grass growth not too rank. Oak colonised the whole range of site types.

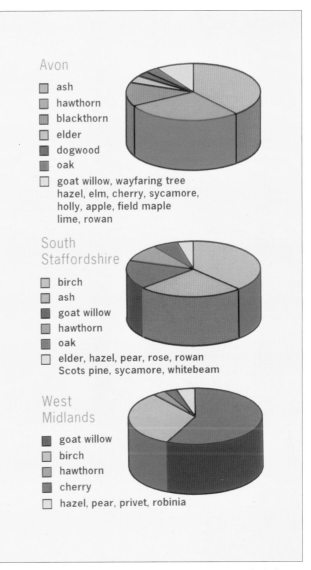

Figure 6.2 Species mix of colonisation in Avon (lightly urbanised), South Staffordshire (moderately urbanised) and the West Midlands (heavily urbanised) from a Forestry Commission Research Division survey of abandoned sites.

Site conditions can be modified to increase the likelihood of colonisation. Apart from direct seeding, little can be done to increase the supply of seed to a site, although there is evidence that bird perches can significantly increase the rate of colonisation of bird-dispersed species like hawthorn, holly and elder. Possibly of more benefit is removal of rank vegetation by cultivation, harrowing or herbicides, or reducing fertility by topsoil stripping. However, success is still not guaranteed because of other factors like seed supply, seed predation and site chemical conditions, and operations may need to be continued over several years before colonisation occurs and trees establish.

William Ellis wrote in 1745 that colonisation should be used primarily to augment rather than create woodlands, and this advice remains relevant today. When you find colonisation on a planting site incorporate it into the design if possible. Dense colonisation may need respacing and thinning to allow light penetration and promote structural diversity (Chapter 7, Silvicultural management and regeneration of mature woodlands). Where there is no woody colonisation consider leaving some land unplanted and managing it to encourage colonisation. Foster colonisation between the planted trees and use it to increase species diversity and to break up the planting pattern (Chapter 5, Vegetation management between trees).

Abandoned sites that have been colonised and have developed into woodland can be very important to urban amenity and landscape; in a recent survey undertaken by the Black Country Urban Forestry Unit natural colonisation was found to be the origin of 35% of the woodland in the West Midlands Borough of Sandwell. Unfortunately, the value of existing naturally colonised woodlands is often not recognised, possibly because they have not been subject to the normal management processes. Many are lost to development, or even to expensive landscaping schemes.

## Direct seeding

In some circumstances, woodlands can be created using seed rather than young trees. This can be done in two main ways:

- broadcasting or drilling tree seed (with or without an agricultural crop such as barley or linseed); and
- planting a small number of seeds in specific planting positions (dibbling).

Information on quantities of seed required is rather scanty, but Table 6.2 gives provisional recommendations taking into account likely germination success in field conditions and the likely losses of seed and seedlings by predation and weed competition. Insist on a certificate of germination or viability from commercial seed suppliers and send samples of locally collected seed to a tree seed testing station for evaluation. You can then adjust the sowing densities in Table 6.2 according to the germination quality of your seed.

Woodland establishment by direct seeding is often more expensive, and certainly less reliable, than planting. The large volume of seed required may necessitate the use of imported material, and it does not usually offer the best use of locally collected seed. Direct sowing in cultivated strips reduces seed requirement by 30%, and direct sowing by dibbling can reduce seed requirement by 75% but is much more labour intensive. However, the lower seed numbers make these methods more prone to failure, although the chances of success can be improved by using chitted (already germinated)

Plate 6.3a  Direct seeding of acorns using modified agricultural equipment.

Plate 6.3b  Direct sown oak under a cover crop of wheat.

**Table 6.2  Seed requirements and cost for woodland establishment by direct sowing**

| Species | Germination (%) | Direct sowing densities (kg per ha) | Cost of seed (£ per ha 1993) |
|---|---|---|---|
| Ash | 60 | 23 | 180 |
| Beech | 50 | 87 | 960 |
| Birch | 20 | 3 | 370 |
| Common alder | 40 | 4 | 370 |
| European larch | 35 | 2 | 500 |
| Field maple | 30 | 245 | 2940 |
| Hazel | 70 | 3000 | 7200 |
| Hornbeam | 55 | 16 | 410 |
| Norway spruce | 75 | 1 | 150 |
| Pedunculate oak | 65 | 570 | 1850 |
| Scots pine | 70 | 1 | 170 |
| Sessile oak | 57 | 560 | 1960 |
| Sycamore | 45 | 58 | 435 |
| Wild cherry | 40 | 540 | 6480 |

seed and treeshelters to protect selected seedlings and allow weed control (Plate 6.4).

Success is most likely with large-seeded species, and species which are not deeply dormant. In a recent example of direct seeding on agricultural land, large seeded species made up 21% of the seed mix but constituted 47% of the seedlings after the first growing season (Figure 6.3). Ash seeds, which are deeply dormant, made up 35% of the seed mix but only 1% of the seedlings after one year. More ash may germinate in the second season, but by this time weed competition will probably be intense, even where graminicides are used. Even on this fertile arable site, only 6.5% of the seed produced seedlings by the end of the first growing season. Stocking is likely to decrease over subsequent seasons as mammal damage and weed competition take their toll.

John Mortimer, in his book of 1708, recommended the use of a cover crop for direct sowing of ash keys and made all the major points that should be considered with such a system today:

*'But if you would make a wood of them* (ash keys) *at once, dig or plough up a parcel of land and prepare it as for corn* (prepare a seed bed)*; only if you plough it give it a summers fallowing to kill and rot the turf* (take steps to eliminate weeds before sowing)*, ploughing of it as deep as you can, and with your corn, especially oats, sow your ash keys, and at harvest taking off your crop of corn the next spring you will find it covered with young ashes, which by reason of their small growth the first year should be kept well weeded* (the importance of weed control) *and well secured from cattle, who are very desirous of cropping them* (the need to control browsing animals)*, the second year they will strike root, and quickly surmount what impediments they may meet.'*

John Mortimer painted a very optimistic picture of the potential of direct seeding on the basis that browsing and weed competition will be controlled, but in practice many more recent attempts to use it have met with failure, principally due to the following:

- slow emergence of tree seed which results in high seed losses by predation, desiccation and shading;

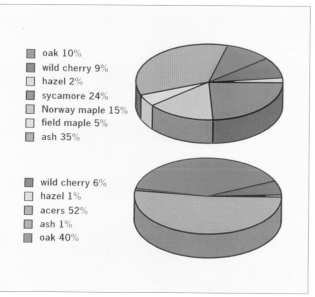

Figure 6.3 Tree seed a) sown (103 300 seeds per ha = 100%) and b) recorded after one growing season (6705 seedlings per ha = 100%)

Plate 6.4 Chitted ash seed inside a treeshelter, planted at five keys per planting position. Individual tree protection is used to protect seeds and seedlings from predation and to make them easier to locate and weed. (*41050*)

## Prescription for the direct sowing of tree seed

1  Kill weeds on site in the summer before sowing using foliar-acting, rather than residual, herbicides.

2  Cultivate to relieve compaction and create a seed bed.

3  Repeat herbicide application if recolonisation of woods occurs after cultivation.

4  Fence out browsing animals (domestic stock, deer, hares, rabbits) if present.

5  Sow freshly collected seed in October or November. Sow bought-in seed in March if it has been pre-treated to break dormancy.

6  Harrow soon after sowing to bury seed into mineral soil for protection against predation and weather extremes.

7  Use graminicides (herbicides that kill only grasses) to control aggressive grasses after seedling emergence. Other herbicides will also kill tree seedlings.

8  If fencing is not undertaken, selected seedlings can be protected with treeshelters.

# For more information

## Publications

Gordon, A. G. (1992). *Seed manual for forest trees.* Forestry Commission Bulletin 83. HMSO, London.

Putwain, P. D. and Evans, B. E. (1992). Experimental creation of naturalistic amenity woodland with fertiliser and herbicide management plus lupin companion plants. *Aspects of Applied Biology 29: Vegetation management in forestry, amenity and conservation areas.* pp. 179–186.

Schlich, W. (1904). *Schlich's manual of forestry Vol II: Silviculture.* Third edition. Bradbury, Agnew and Co., London.

Stevens, F. R. W., Thompson, D. A. and Gosling, P. G. (1990). *Research experience in direct sowing for lowland plantation establishment.* Research Information Note 184. Forestry Commission, Edinburgh.

## Advice

Seed testing: The Official Seed Testing Station for trees and shrubs is at the Forestry Commission's Research Station, Alice Holt Lodge, Farnham, Surrey GU10 4LH.

- unpredictability of germination;
- difficulties of weed control and slow early growth relative to competing vegetation which leads to intense competition for water, nutrients and light;
- loss of establishing seedlings from animal pests.

# 7 Managing existing woodlands

## The management plan

Woodland planting and establishment will be guided by the written specification (Chapter 4, Drafting a specification), which should include a review date, usually five years after planting, as a prompt to formulate the first five-year management plan for the established woodland. If the original objectives for a woodland are to be achieved this continuity of management planning is essential as aspects of the design need to be implemented and particular management operations undertaken at different stages in the life of the woodland (Chapter 4, Practical woodland design).

The structure of a management plan should broadly follow that of the initial specification and some information can be transferred from the speci-

fication where one exists. Reiterate or, if necessary, modify the objectives for management and outline clearly the management needed in the next five years to enable the woodland to meet these objectives. Remember to include the next five-year review date. The management plan need not be long and its structure can be adapted to meet the

**Essential elements of a woodland management plan**

1 Site name, location and grid reference.
2 Identification of project coordinator.
3 Background and description of the site.
4 Objectives of woodland management on the site, listed by priority.
5 Rationale for management – woodland type and desired stand characteristics for each part of the woodland.
6 Open space – objectives for, and management of, open space within the wood.
7 Detail of silvicultural operations (with supporting maps as necessary).
8 Timing of operations within the five-year plan period.
9 Responsibilities.
10 Resource requirement and sources.
11 Review date – usually after five years.
12 Distribution list.

needs of a particular woodland. Use maps to convey clearly and concisely spatial information about the woodland and proposed operations.

## Initiating a silvicultural system

When designing a woodland you will need to consider the silvicultural system that is most appropriate for achieving the objectives, and the management operations needed for its introduction. Most urban woodlands are managed as high forest, where trees are allowed to grow to their mature height, creating relatively even-aged stands. Because this woodland type tends to develop without intervention it does not need specific early management for

Plate 7.1   An ash tree coppiced when five years old. (*40972*)

its initiation. The other sections in this chapter focus on the management and regeneration of high forest woodlands.

### Coppice

Coppice is produced by coppicing: cutting near the base of the stem and allowing the regrowth of a number of shoots from the cut stump. Coppicing can be used to increase woodland structural diversity and is a good way of involving local people in woodland management. It has the potential to produce wood for a variety of urban uses if even-sized poles can be produced from a suitable species in sufficient quantity to interest a user (Chapter 2, A long-term perspective). The Freckland Wood case study shows how plans have been developed for coppicing in a new urban edge woodland (Chapter 9, The final specification).

To initiate a coppice system in a recently established woodland, divide the area into a number of coupes to be cut at different times. Coupes can be shaped according to the design objectives but should be at least 0.1 ha (0.5 ha if wood is to be commercially coppiced). Most urban woodlands will be too small to support an annual cut on a rotation of 10 to 20 years (Table 7.1) and so the appropriate number of coupes should be divided by the proposed rotation length to determine the required interval between cutting (for example, if 10 ha are to be cut on a 20-year rotation using 1 ha coupe, one coupe will be cut every two years).

The first coppice coupe can be cut at the end of the establishment phase (Plate 7.1), although cutting can be delayed until stems become saleable if income is important. Coppicing can be done at any time of year although you should avoid the bird nesting season, and it is easier when there is no foliage on the trees. Cut as close to the ground as

**Table 7.1  Products and rotations for coppice** (adapted from Evans, 1984)

| Species | Rotation (years) | Stools/ha | Products |
|---|---|---|---|
| Alder | 10–15 | 1100–1500 | Charcoal, turnery, fuel-wood, wood-chips. |
| Ash | 10–25 | 750–1500 | Turnery, thatching sways, tool handles, split rails, fuel-wood, wood-chips. |
| Birch | 15–25 | 750–1100 | Turnery, horse jumps, fuel-wood, wood-chips. |
| Hazel | 6–9 | 1500–2000 | Hurdles, thatching spars, pea and bean sticks, hedge-laying stakes, wood-chips. |
| Oak | 30 | 600 | Fencing, fuel-wood, tan bark, charcoal, wood-chips. |
| Other hardwoods and mixed coppice | 20–25 | 750–900 | Fuel-wood, pulp, turnery, wood-chips. |
| Sweet chestnut | 15 | 1100 | Stakes, fence palings, hop poles, fuel-wood, wood-chips. |
| Sycamore | 10–20 | 900–1500 | Turnery, fuel-wood, wood-chips. |

possible to encourage coppice shoots from the root collar to improve the stability of the coppice stool. The angle of cut appears to have no effect on the success of shoot initiation. Coppice regrowth is vulnerable to deer and rabbit browsing for the first two or three years and you may need to exclude them or control animal numbers.

## Coppice with standards

Coppice with standards is a two-storey management system where among the coppice (underwood) some trees (standards) are grown on for larger size timber. The overstorey of standards should not be even-aged and, at each coppicing, some mature standards should be felled and a few new ones established by planting or natural regeneration. Regular spacing of standards is not important but they should cast only light shade, which rules out the use of beech and limits numbers to, at most, 100 per ha. More than 30% canopy cover reduces coppice vigour and can result in the death of freshly coppiced stools.

Coppice-with-standard management is appropriate for ancient semi-natural woodlands where this has been the traditional management system. However, in secondary woodland the complexity of management and possible negative landscape impact means that it should only be used where it will be particularly beneficial. A more practical way of achieving structural diversity is to create a mosaic of coppice coupes and stands of high forest at a scale appropriate to the woodland. This simplifies management and is less vulnerable to neglect.

## Wood-pasture

Wood-pasture is a traditional system of agro-forestry where wood is produced on land that is grazed. Wood-pastures differ widely in appearance according to the amount of grazing and the method chosen to control it: they can vary from open grass-land with scattered trees to woodland. Many wood-pastures involve pollarding, the practice of cutting a tree at 2 to 5 m above the ground, leaving a permanent base called a bolling. Once cut, the tree is able to resprout above the reach of grazing animals.

Wood-pasture will rarely be a practical possibility in urban situations but there may be opportunities for using pollarding to manage widely spaced trees in amenity grassland. Pollards can be created from recently planted trees by cutting out the leading shoot and pruning lower branches once the tree is taller than the desired bolling height. When the remaining branches have grown to a useable size the tree can be pollarded. This approach will be most effective on species that have poor leading shoot dominance such as oak, beech and hornbeam. Alternatively, trees can be left until 25 to 35 years old, by which time the branches removed by pollarding will be large enough to be sold or used.

# Silvicultural management of recently established woodlands

Establishment is considered to be complete when trees are growing vigorously without the need for regular maintenance. However, the need for active management does not end at tree establishment.

Even newly established woodlands can offer amenity, recreation, conservation and landscape benefits, but these can only be fully realised by sensitive and well-timed management. If woodlands are neglected at this stage, not only will their present and future value be reduced but the cost of management in later years could be unduly high (and hence the likelihood of it taking place low).

The silvicultural operations required during the first management-plan period will depend on the condition of the woodland at the end of the establishment phase and desired woodland characteristics. If survival and growth rates have been poor, some areas will need to be replanted, and management options to develop the woodland further will be limited. In this case the first management plan will be very similar to the initial specification. If the woodland is well stocked and vigorous, the specified operations will relate initially to manipulating species composition and increasing structural diversity.

## Manipulating species composition

Intervention will generally be aimed at increasing species diversity by planting shrub and understorey species, by favouring natural colonisation that may be occurring, or by removing trees of a dominant species where they threaten to shade out a preferred species (Chapter 4, The importance of robustness). Colonisation by invasive or inappropriate species may need to be removed, particularly if a clearly defined woodland type is desired.

## Increasing structural diversity

Without active management planted woodlands can become homogeneous in structure. The dense tree canopy cuts out light to the woodland floor, restricting understorey, shrub and field-layer development.

This is rarely desirable in urban woodlands. Careful design of species layout can give woodland inherent structural diversity with different tree species varying in their form, growth rate and ultimate size. Choice of silvicultural system will also have a profound influence on structural diversity. In woodlands where a predominantly high-forest system is to be used structural diversity can be enhanced by gap creation or enlargement, cleaning (removal of dense, choking understorey growth), small scale coppicing and fostering of natural colonisation. The development of a graded woodland edge can be encouraged by delayed shrub planting and the use of differential fertiliser regimes on impoverished sites, with the trees nearest the woodland edge not receiving fertiliser.

## Thinning

As a high-forest woodland gets older, thinning becomes the main way of manipulating stand structure and species composition. Thinning encourages the growth of remaining trees and increases the amount of light penetrating the canopy to the benefit of the understorey, shrub and field layers. The decisions that must be made when planning thinning operations are:

- when to start thinning;
- what proportion of the trees to remove;
- how to decide which trees to remove; and
- how often to thin.

These decisions usually involve compromise between the silvicultural ideal (frequent, light, selective thinning) and the need to minimise the net cost (or maximise net income) from thinning (infrequent, heavy, systematic thinning).

Plate 7.2 A broadleaved stand being thinned to maintain an open canopy with good light penetration. (*40984*)

## When to start thinning

In woodlands for timber, thinning broadleaved stands normally starts when trees reach 10 m in height, usually between age 15 and 25, depending on species and growth rate. However, if creation of diverse, attractive woodlands is a high priority, use the degree of ground flora suppression by shading as your guide to when to start thinning. In well-stocked urban woodlands thinning should start early to maintain light penetration to the woodland floor for flora development. However, woodlands planted at wide spacings with poor survival may not need to be thinned for 30 years.

## What proportion of trees to remove

In broadleaved woodland the importance of removing a particular proportion of the trees is less than with conifers as the primary objective of thinning is to improve the remaining woodland rather than to maximise total timber production. However, the cost of (or potential income from) thinning will still be an important consideration in urban woodlands and so it should be heavy enough to make the operation worth while. In a young woodland each thinning operation should remove about 25% of the trees, although after five or so thinning operations this should be reduced to 15%. At this rate of tree removal, most thinning operations should yield between 20 and 45 $m^3$ of wood per ha.

In dense young stands it may not be cost effective to remove the wood, which can be left on the woodland floor. In this case, the proportion of trees removed can be lower than would otherwise be acceptable.

## How to decide which trees to remove

Which trees are removed in a thinning operation depends on:

- the type of woodland;
- the objectives for management; and
- the resources available for woodland management.

Conifer stands tend to be fairly uniform and so tree removal in woodlands containing conifers can be systematic for the first one or two thinning operations in the knowledge that most conifers that remain will be as able to meet the objectives for planting as those that were removed. Systematic methods include removing whole rows of trees or removing every fourth tree, and are the cheapest method of thinning.

Most broadleaved woodlands contain trees which vary in their ability to meet specified objectives, and so thinning operations should be selective, in order to leave the most desirable trees. Where timber production is the main objective thinning will favour healthy, straight crop trees of a species with valuable timber (Chapter 8, Woodlands for timber production). Where conservation is the main objective thinning will favour native trees appropriate to the site, trees that will form a diverse woodland structure and that offer a range of niches for wildlife (for example dead branches and cavities) (Chapter 8, Woodlands for wildlife). In multi-purpose woodlands for use by local people the choice of trees to remove will lay between these two extremes. Consider thinning to favour several hundred good timber trees per hectare whilst thinning to enhance diversity in the rest of the stand.

If the tree selection criteria you set are very specific you may need to mark the trees for removal prior to thinning. For less exacting criteria a sample area can be marked, and when using experienced foresters a 'feller-selection' system can be used after a site briefing.

## How often to thin

After receiving its first thinning a woodland can be left until the tree crowns are fully touching. By this time the degree of shading will start to become detrimental to the ground flora, and the degree of overcrowding detrimental to favoured trees. Most broadleaved stands require thinning every 5 to 10 years, although for mature stands 10 to 15 years is adequate as tree growth rates tend to decline.

## Neglected woodlands

It may occasionally be in the interest of specific conservation objectives to withdraw management completely from all or part of a wood. However, woodlands that have not received periodic thinning tend to become dark, impenetrable and ill suited to meeting amenity, wildlife or timber production objectives. Active management by thinning or coppicing should be a priority in these woodlands despite the legacy of neglect resulting in higher costs and lower income.

Thinning neglected stands is expensive as access is difficult and cut trees get caught in the crowns of surrounding trees. Potential income is low as overcrowding results in a large number of small spindly trees. Heavy thinning of over stocked woodland can increase the risk of wind damage, dieback, snow-break, development of epicormic branches and damage to remaining trees during the harvesting operation. Remove only 10 to 15% of trees at each thinning to minimise these risks. It may take two or three light thinning operations over a number of years before a woodland is fully restored.

If the neglected woodland is reaching maturity the response to thinning will be dependent on the species. For example, ash is very poor in its response when crowns have become small due to overcrowding, whilst oak is generally able to expand its crown after thinning provided crown dieback has not begun. The risk of damage after thinning is higher in woodland reaching maturity and so you should consider starting group selection felling and regeneration early with the aim of achieving a gradual replacement of the neglected stand.

# Silvicultural management and regeneration of mature woodlands

As high-forest woodlands approach maturity, you must plan to perpetuate them. In some stands trees should be left until the end of their natural life for wildlife and as objects of history and beauty. However, failure to take any action to regenerate a woodland will lead to a loss of structural diversity and vulnerability to the effects of windblow. In addition, over-mature trees may pose an unacceptable hazard in heavily used woodlands.

## Planting or natural regeneration?

Planting is necessary if desired species are not already on site or if it is important to achieve rapid and complete restocking. Natural regeneration is often more difficult and less reliable than planting but may be favoured when:

- the parent species are suitable;
- there is already some regeneration taking place;
- there is no urgency to fell and restock in the same year; and
- conservation of local genetic stock is important.

Natural regeneration occurring before or soon after felling can be used in two ways:

- if there is a sufficient stocking of acceptable species, favour them by weeding, cleaning and, where appropriate, individual tree protection;

- use regeneration of less desirable species to add robustness (Chapter 4, The importance of robustness) and to give shelter to widely spaced planted trees.

## Silvicultural systems for woodland regeneration

Clear cutting (Figure 7.1a) has been the traditional system of regenerating broadleaved high forest in Britain and coupes tend to be between 1 and 4 ha. Clear cutting is usually followed by replanting because natural regeneration over such large areas rarely results in adequate stocking of desirable species. Species with light, windblown seed such as goat willow and birch are likely to be first to colonise (Chapter 6, Natural colonisation).

Group selection (Figure 7.1b) will often be the best way to regenerate urban high-forest woodlands because it offers the potential to maintain the benefits of mature woodland on a site in perpetuity. Groups of between 0.1 and 0.5 ha are felled, which are large enough to allow the regeneration of light-demanding species. When regeneration has occurred, the group can be enlarged and new ones created. The smallest group felling should create a gap with a diameter at least twice the height of adjacent trees. The woodland is divided up into an appropriate number of coupes which will be felled and regenerated over a planned time period. Large woodlands may warrant the felling and regeneration of two or more coupes a year, whilst smaller woodlands may warrant the felling of only one coupe every five years. Whilst harvesting costs are relatively high with small areas of felling, if the stand has been well managed the value of the trees removed may be considerable.

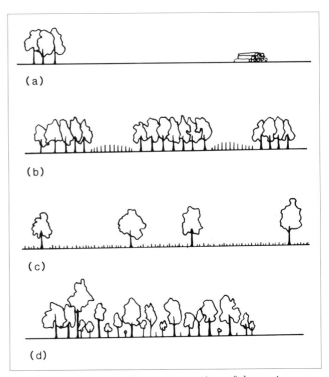

Figure 7.1 Diagrammatic representation of the main woodland regeneration systems.

The shelterwood system (Figure 7.1c) involves partially felling a stand to leave a scattered overstorey of seed bearing trees. For light-demanding species such as oak, ash and sycamore six to ten metres should be left between remaining crowns. For beech the gap size can be reduced to four metres. The overstorey reduces the effect of frost and exposure on regeneration and can shade out aggressive weed growth. With ash, alder, birch, cherry and sycamore the overstorey should be removed three to four years after regeneration has occurred to ensure that sufficient light reaches the young trees. Overstorey removal over oak should be in five to seven years in two stages and for beech phased removal over 15 years is possible. This system is little used in Britain but is particularly suitable for regenerating species with heavy seeds such as beech and oak.

Individual tree selection (Figure 7.1d) is a method for creating irregular (uneven-aged) woodlands which contain an intimate mixture of age classes. Young trees, whether naturally regenerated or planted, must be of a shade-tolerant species as the canopy is never completely opened up; the system is classically used for regenerating beech. Because management is expensive and difficult, this system is usually suitable only for the smallest woodlands where group systems are not feasible, and where side light encourages regeneration.

## Preparing for natural regeneration

The silvicultural requirements for natural regeneration are:

- plentiful seed;
- sparse ground vegetation;
- freedom from browsing animals; and
- low levels of weed competition during the regeneration period.

Any patches of existing regeneration should be used as focal points for group felling. If possible fell after

**Table 7.2  Seed production of broadleaved trees in Britain** (from Evans, 1988)

| Species | Minimum seed bearing age (years) | Average interval between large seed crops | Age after which seed production begins to decline | Time of seed fall |
|---|---|---|---|---|
| Common alder | 15–25 | 2–3 | 60 | Sept–Mar |
| Ash | 20–30 | 3–5 | 100 | Sept–Mar |
| Beech | 50–60 | 5–15 | 160 | Sept–Nov |
| Birch | 15 | 1–3 | 60 | Aug–Jan |
| Cherry | 10 | 1–3 | 100 | July–Aug |
| Norway maple | 25–30 | 1–3 | 100 | Oct–Feb |
| Pedunculate oak | 40–50 | 3–6 | 160 | Nov |
| Sessile oak | 40–50 | 2–5 | 160 | Nov |
| Sycamore | 25–30 | 1–3 | 100 | Sept–Oct |

Plate 7.3a  Prolific natural regeneration of beech has been achieved in a well-thinned beech stand at Haigh Hall near Wigan . . .

Plate 7.3b  . . . but where visitor pressure is intense, soils are compacted and eroded and natural regeneration is not forthcoming.

a good seed year when there should be an abundance of seed on the ground. If felling is in a poor seed year, it may be best to delay treatment of the woodland floor until after a good seed year (Table 7.2). An assessment of the developing seed crop can be made with binoculars in late June.

Compacted, eroded or waterlogged soils are inhospitable to germination and deep cultivation and drainage may be needed to encourage natural regeneration. If visitor pressure is intense, site users may need to be diverted away from the area to be regenerated (Plates 7.3 a and b). The likelihood of successful natural regeneration is increased by scarification or disc ploughing to create a seedbed of loosened mineral soil, and by removal of competing vegetation. If these are achieved by late summer, before seed fall, the seed will become covered by leaf litter in the autumn, creating ideal conditions for germination. Some species (such as ash, field maple and hazel) may remain dormant for a year and so a lack of regeneration in the first year might be misleading.

Respacing is the removal of excess natural regeneration to favour selected stems (Plate 7.4). Abundant regeneration that is not respaced will develop into dense impenetrable woodland. Respacing is best done with a clearing saw once regeneration is about 2.5 m tall. Dense regeneration should be respaced in stages over two or three years to reach the target tree density (2500 to 4500 trees per ha) without risking stand instability and vigorous coppice regrowth from the cut stems, which could suppress the selected trees.

## Protection of existing woodlands

### Damage from mammals

Control of damage from deer, rabbits, hares and voles is essential for successful regeneration (Plate 7.5) or coppice regrowth (Chapter 5, Tree protection). Established trees can be seriously damaged or killed from bark stripping by grey squirrels, rabbits, deer and livestock (Table 7.3). In addition, fraying damage (the removal of bark from the stems and branches of young trees by male deer rubbing the velvet from their antlers or territory marking in preparation for the rut) can be locally intense. The main fraying period for roe deer is March to August and for other species mid July to mid September. Rabbits, deer or livestock must be fenced out or reduced in number if causing serious damage. Grey squirrels are more difficult to control. The recommended method, where damage is compromising the objectives of the woodland, and where red squirrels are not present, is poisoning with 0.2 %

Plate 7.4 A clearing saw is invaluable for respacing naturally seeded trees and preventing the suppression of the preferred trees in recently established or regenerated woodlands. (*40983*)

warfarin on wheat dispensed from purpose designed hoppers. Other forms of control – shooting and trapping – are less effective.

Plate 7.5 Relieving browsing pressure by fencing this woodland glade has resulted in an abundance of naturally seeded trees.

The issue of controlling mammal damage is complicated in urban woodlands by the need to consider woodland users and the urban situation.

- Disturbance by woodland users will tend to reduce the occurrence of mammal damage.
- Woodland animals are a part of the attraction of woodland.
- Controlling animal numbers by poisoning, shooting, trapping or gassing may be impossible because of the intensity of public use, or undesirable because of strong local feeling.
- The risk of vandalism to fences or theft of netting can make fencing an unreliable form of control, and certainly necessitates regular fence inspection and prompt replacement of stolen or damaged sections.
- Minimising the use of fencing benefits public access and enjoyment.
- Individual tree protection can increase vandalism of the trees (Chapter 4, Practical woodland design) and can leave trees vulnerable to damage if removed.

In many urban woodlands these factors will result in a policy of no control, tree damage and limitation of management options being accepted as the opportunity cost.

## Fire

Fire risk (likelihood of a fire starting) is high for much of the time in many urban woodlands and is directly linked to the intensity of public use. Fire hazard (susceptibility of vegetation to burn if a fire does occur) is highest:

- during prolonged periods of dry weather, particularly in early spring and late summer when there is a lot of dead vegetation present; and

- in newly established or restocked woodland where canopy closure has not yet occurred and there are continuous stretches of dense ground vegetation (and large volumes of branch-wood on restock sites).

Wild-fires are suprisingly difficult to start at most times of the year and damage is likely to be restricted to a few trees only (Plate 7.6). The value of mowing inter-row vegetation over the whole planted area to reduce the impact of deliberate fire raising is debatable. Whilst the fire hazard can be reduced in this way, the risk of localised outbreaks of fire may be considered acceptable when balanced against the expense and disadvantages of mowing (Chapter 5, Vegetation management between trees) and the fact that most broadleaved species will

**Table 7.3  Bark stripping damage to established trees** (adapted from Kerr and Evans, 1993)

| Mammal | Tree species | Size/age | Description of damage | Time of year |
|---|---|---|---|---|
| Grey squirrel | Beech and sycamore are most susceptible but all species can be damaged | 10- to 40- year old trees | Bark stripping is most serious on the stem but can occur on root spurs or on the branches of older trees. Incisor marks are 1.5 mm wide in pairs, running parallel along branches and vertically on stems. | May to mid Aug |
| Rabbits | All, but thin-barked species such as ash and sycamore are most susceptible | All | Bark stripping on root spurs and lower stems up to 50 cm. Incisor marks are 3 to 4 mm wide in pairs, usually running diagonally across the stem. | Winter to early spring |
| Deer | All | 10- to 30- year old trees | Produces characteristic 'stripped wallpaper' appearance. The lower incisor is used to bite into the tree and the bark is pulled upwards leaving vertical teeth marks at the base of the wound. Teeth marks are 6.5 mm to a maximum height of 1.1 m. | Jan to early spring |
| Livestock | All | All | Severe and sometimes complete stripping of bark from ground level to maximum browse height for animal. | Any time but especially winter |

Plate 7.6 Wild-running fires are relatively rare and where they do occur many broadleaved tree species will subsequently resprout.

resprout after a running ground fire so damage caused will often be temporary. However, the likelihood of accidental fires can be reduced by mowing rides and five metres into tree planting adjacent to rides, in order to reduce the bulk of combustible material during times of high fire hazard.

## For more information

### Publications

Evans, J. (1984). *Silviculture of broadleaved woodland.* Forestry Commission Bulletin 62. HMSO, London.

Evans, J. (1988). *Natural regeneration of broadleaves.* Forestry Commission Bulletin 78. HMSO, London.

Hart, C. (1991). *Practical forestry for the agent and surveyor.* Alan Sutton, Stroud.

Hibberd, B. G. (1991). *Forestry practice.* Forestry Commission Handbook 6. HMSO, London.

Kerr, G. and Evans, J. (1993). *Growing broadleaves for timber.* Forestry Commission Handbook 9. HMSO, London.

Matthews, J. D. (1990). *Silvicultural systems.* Clarendon Press, Oxford.

Rackham, O. (1980). *Ancient woodland: its history, vegetation and uses in England.* Edward Arnold, London.

Rollinson, T. J. D. (1988). *Thinning control.* Forestry Commission Field Book 2. HMSO, London.

### Advice

National Small Woods Association, Hall Farm House, Preston Capes, Northamptonshire, NN11 6TA. (01327) 36387.

Coppice Association, Eastern Cottage, Main Road, Toft, Bourne, Lincolnshire, PE10 0JT. (01778) 33470.

# 8  Woodlands for particular uses

Most woodlands are able to yield some benefits for landscape, recreation, wildlife and timber production even if not managed to those ends. However, where specific objectives have been set, targeted design and management can greatly increase the potential of the woodland. Woodland landscape design is comprehensively covered in the Forestry Commission's *Community woodland design guidelines* and *Lowland landscape design guidelines* so is not considered in detail in this chapter.

## Woodlands for recreation and amenity

### What are appropriate activities?

Woodlands are capable of supporting a wide range of leisure activities and the owner or manager must decide which activities are appropriate, depending on the following considerations.

- **The objectives and attitude of the manager.** Many public landowners will see provision for recreation and amenity as the primary objective of management. Private landowners may be encouraged to allow and provide for access but generally this will be a secondary objective of management. Landowners on the urban edge may not be able to prevent access and making provision for controlled access may divert people from sensitive areas and reduce vandalism and antisocial behaviour.

- **The size and characteristics of the woodland.** This will define the 'carrying capacity' of the woodland, the types of activities that would be feasible and the extent to which a range of recreation and amenity related demands can be met. Opportunities will be greatest in large, mature, diverse woodlands that are linked well with a wider recreational network (Chapter 2, Providing a recreation network).

- **Preferences of existing woodland users.** The preferences of existing woodland users can be established by survey, informal conversations and evidence of activities. Appropriate provision for recreation and amenity will depend on the number and type of people using the wood and the average duration of stay.

- **Views and preferences of local people.** If new woodlands have been established or access only recently liberalised there is less likely to be a body of users to consult. Local people can be consulted on what would attract them to the woodland and what activities they would find antisocial.

Plate 8.1 Archery is a recreation requiring the attributes of woodland for functional rather than aesthetic reasons. (*18846*)

Plate 8.2 Many activities are undertaken in woodland simply because it is a nice place to be.

- **Approaches from local clubs or hobby groups.**
The demand for formal recreational activities is usually manifest in approaches from local clubs.

## Recreation

Some activities can be conveniently located in woodlands but derive only a secondary benefit from the aesthetic quality of the surroundings. The focus of attention is the activity itself rather than the environment in which it takes place. Car rallying takes place in large forests mainly because of the presence of suitable forest tracks; archery takes place in woodlands as the trees present a barrier for stray arrows; paint-balling takes place in woodlands because they provide suitable terrain and cover. For the purposes of this Handbook these are termed recreational activities and are characteristically formal, active, organised, guided and gregarious.

## Amenity

Some activities are based on enjoyment of the woodland environment and so depend on the aesthetic qualities of the woodland. The enjoyment derived from walking, picnicking, nature watching and photography depend to a large extent on the aesthetic qualities of the surroundings. For the purposes of this Handbook these are referred to as amenity and are characteristically informal, passive, unorganised, unguided and solitary.

Of course, the division between activity-oriented recreation and environment-oriented amenity is hazy and activities generally contain an element of both. Some activities such as pony-trekking and cycling fall towards the middle of this continuum, with the enjoyment of the leisure experience coming equally from the activity itself and the environment in which it takes place.

## Managing woodland for recreation and amenity

The emphasis of woodland management for recreation will be to provide the facilities required for the activity (roads for rallying, a barrier of trees for archery, and suitable cover for paint-balling). Recreation management will be infrastructure oriented in order to cater for organised groups which need ample parking space and possibly toilet facilities. There will often be less need for on-site interpretation as people are guided to and informed about the activity by organisers.

Where recreational activities predominate, the woodland itself can be managed for other objectives with relatively few concessions being required to facilitate the particular activity. Because most woodlands have inherent aesthetic qualities, whatever the objectives of management the woodland will provide a pleasing backdrop to the recreational activity.

The emphasis of woodland amenity management will be to provide a conducive environment for amenity related activities. Recent research confirms that people value variety and contrasts in woodland (Chapter 4, Practical woodland design). Features such as ponds, streams, glades and varied relief are attractive and valuable as they greatly enhance variety and provide strong contrasts. Variety and contrasts within the wooded area can be increased by:

- using species of contrasting colour and form;
- maximising the structural diversity of the woodland;
- varying the scale of stands through the woodland; and
- careful planning of rides and open space to give a variety of views and visual contrasts.

Viewing wildlife, particularly birds, mammals, butterflies and woodland flowers, is an important aspect of the amenity value of woodland. A study on the recreation and amenity value of forests found that, on average, 38% of the value of a woodland visit was ascribed to seeing or hoping to see wildlife. Management practices that encourage and protect attractive flora and fauna will increase the amenity value of a woodland.

The provision of some facilities can greatly improve the value of woodlands for amenity.

Plate 8.4 Glimpsing a wild animal such as this roe deer adds a lot to the pleasure derived from woodlands.

Plate 8.3 Features such as ponds greatly enhance the amenity value of woodland, as well as providing a diversity of opportunities for wildlife.

Because visits for amenity are characteristically informal, passive, unorganised, unguided and solitary, on-site interpretation and way-marked routes are usually appreciated. Picnic tables, barbecue grates, areas suitable for games or viewing hides may be as attractive to many visitors as the woodland environment itself. Judgement and careful design is always needed to balance the benefits of

Plate 8.5   A surface suitable for wheelchairs and seating has been provided without compromising the aesthetic qualities of the woodland.

facilities against the effect they will have on the aesthetic qualities of the woodland.

Reconciling various uses and objectives in multipurpose woodlands can become particularly difficult where visitor pressure is intense. This makes the clear definition and prioritising of objectives particularly important (Chapter 4, Setting objectives and priorities). Formal recreational activities, whilst they are taking place, may not be compatible with other recreation and amenity uses. Zoning can be used in large woodlands to keep incompatible activities apart. In smaller woodlands it will generally be most appropriate to encourage unobtrusive amenity related activities, as intensive use for specific recreational activities may preclude informal amenity use for much of the time.

## Design with user safety in mind

The use and enjoyment of urban woodlands can be severely restricted for wide sections of the community, for both practical and perceptual reasons of safety. Statistics show that the frequency of violent attacks in parks and woodlands is considerably lower than in built-up areas. Nonetheless, the design of urban woodlands should try to overcome the fear resulting from actual and perceived risks.

Design and management to reduce people's sense of anxiety and fear can reduce the natural informality of woodland. For this reason it will not be appropriate to attempt to make all woodlands feel totally safe to all sections of the community. Focus measures on sites close to residential areas and at access points to woodlands where public activity is concentrated and where a formal landscape is acceptable. There are a number of design and management issues to consider when designing to maximise safety and perceptions of safety.

Plate 8.6 For many sections of the community, woodlands can be perceived as dark and threatening places. In some locations, increasing feelings of safety must be a high design priority. (*40961*)

- Limiting the number of principal routes within the woodland. This will concentrate site users into a smaller area and therefore increase contact and feelings of safety. Obviously, wilder paths should be available for those wanting to use them.

- Through routes may need to be lit.

- Principal routes should be planned with clear views for fairly long distances. Corners or junctions should be designed to provide maximum visibility. Woodland either side of principal routes should be open with widely spaced trees and little understorey.

- Wide rides reduce the incidence of heavy shadows being cast on the paths during the day.

- Understorey shrubs that are planted adjacent to routes or open spaces should be spiky or thorny to deny cover to potential attackers, and preferably well back from the path.

- Entrances to safe routes will be of special importance and should, as far as possible, relate to safe and busy areas.

- Signs should be used to inform the user about the length and nature of the routes and to make them easy to follow. Signs can also be used to reinforce the perception of the safety by showing the location of places of refuge such as roads and buildings.

- Environmental 'incivilities' such as graffiti, abandoned cars and fly-tipped rubbish should be removed rapidly. They signify to site users a lack of social control and a lack of ownership (Chapter 4, Practical woodland design).
- Specific recreation facilities, such as picnic places, should not be perceived as being hidden in the wood. In some instances the location of facilities at the edge of the wood may help to diffuse the woodland edge, which is seen by many as a barrier between safety and fear.

Woodland managers have a legal responsibility to provide a safe environment for visitors (Chapter 2, Urban woodlands and the law). In mature woodlands formal routes should be regularly inspected for hazards such as dangerous trees or pot-holes in surfaced paths. In heavily used woodlands obvious hazards should be dealt with wherever they are (for example, felling unsafe trees or fencing off steep sided pits). Hazards should be dealt with promptly, and a record kept of inspections and action taken.

## Catering for less-mobile people

Provision for recreation and amenity should be considerate of less-mobile people which includes the disabled, the elderly, the blind, people who are temporarily restricted by accident or pregnancy, as well as people with babies and young children.

Design for less-mobile people should be considered as design for everyone and should be based on six principles.

- Inclusion not exclusion. Less-mobile people are too often excluded from the countryside not by their own limitations but by deficiencies in design and access provision.

Plate 8.7 Where possible access points should be designed to allow access to all sections of the community. Here, the needs of able adults and dogs have been thoughtfully catered for, but what about parents with children in push-chairs!

- Integration not segregation. Less-mobile people are part of the community and do not look for special provision which sets them apart. Whatever is done should be done with the less-mobile person in mind.

- Thought not money. Thought and imagination rather than expensive design solutions are what is often required.

- Promoting recreational opportunities. Less-mobile people need to know where opportunities for them exist.

- Access to the site. If possible, provision for less-mobile people should be linked with the means for them to get to the site.

- Design with less-mobile people, not just for them (Chapter 3, Consultation).

### Income from recreation and amenity

Woodland recreation and amenity will rarely be a viable commercial venture. However, there may be potential to earn income from users to offset some of the cost of management activities. To have potential for income generation a woodland must offer considerable attraction to target customers. The earning potential must be large enough to ensure that income at least exceeds the cost of money collection, if not the cost of provision and maintenance of facilities. The potential for income generation is greatest in large, diverse forests that can accommodate a range of specialist recreational activities for which a charge can be made, and that can attract enough fee-paying visitors to justify capital investment in facilities.

Most urban woodlands will not have sufficient earning potential to warrant charging, even if considerable capital is invested to create an attraction. In addition, an important part of the value and phi-losophy of urban and community forestry is free access and the opportunity to escape from commercial urban pressures into a natural environment. These objectives are generally not compatible with charging or intensive investment in commercial facilities.

## Woodlands for wildlife

Conservation management of woodlands benefits wildlife and the woodland users who experience it. Conservation management should be a high priority in ancient semi-natural woodland, but can greatly enhance the potential for wildlife in any wood. Most woodlands contain a number of habitats, some of which are valuable in their own right. This section focuses on those habitats which are likely to be present or possible to develop in all woodlands, and the factors which affect their conservation value.

**Woodland habitats of importance to wildlife**

- large trees
- standing dead trees
- dying and dead wood
- waterside zones
- deciduous stands
- caves
- cliffs
- areas being naturally colonised
- open spaces
- edges

## Habitat diversity

Diversity of woodland structure increases the number of habitats within a woodland and hence the opportunities for wildlife. There are many opportunities for increasing woodland diversity.

- Landform, site features and site variability will influence vegetation development and provide the basis for a diversity of habitat types.
- The wooded area can encompass and protect a range of unwooded habitats such as grassland, wetland, ponds, streams and bare patches.
- The wooded area can be vertically and spatially diversified through species choice, varying planting density, using natural regeneration, coppic-ing, thinning, group felling (Chapter 7) and periodic cutting of shrubby woodland margins.
- Within stands, habitat diversity can be increased by sensitive management (see 'Stand management for wildlife', below).

Whilst high habitat diversity is valuable, the concept should not be taken too far and should be balanced against the benefits of large areas of a single habitat. Many animals, birds and invertebrates have a minimum area requirement and need a habitat large enough to supply a continuity of food and shelter. In addition, the large areas of a single habitat that may be needed to support viable breeding populations are less vulnerable to catastrophic

Plate 8.8 Woodland design and management should seek to create and enhance structural diversity. This increases the range of habitats in the woodland and the length of internal edges, which tend to be particularly important for wildlife. (*7130*)

disturbances and generally support a greater diversity of specialised species than small fragments of the same habitat.

A diversity of habitat types within a woodland maximises the length of edges between habitats. Edges are of particular importance to wildlife, offering some of the benefits of both habitats. The edge zone between strongly contrasting habitat types should be as wide as possible to avoid abrupt changes.

## The importance of stress

Plants and animals vary in their ability to tolerate stress and disturbance, and the balance of stresses and disturbances will affect the range of organisms a woodland will support. For plants, stress includes infertility, drought, waterlogging, extremes of pH and shading.

For the range of site stresses within which woodland establishment is viable (Chapter 4, Is woodland the best use of the site?), increasing stress tends to increase the diversity and conservation value of a habitat. A newly planted woodland in an arable field with a neutral, fertile, loam soil is a low-stress environment. Hospitable conditions favour the dominance of a few rapidly colonising and fast growing species such as charlock, cleavers, thistles and volunteer cereals, which prevent the colonisation of other less aggressive, but possibly more desirable, species. In contrast, a newly planted woodland on a south facing slope of acidic, infertile colliery shale is a stressed environment. Stress levels prevent colonisation by the few aggressive species, and provide opportunities for a diversity of tolerant successional species which are often of greater conservation value.

Shading is a stress of particular importance in woodlands. Unlike most pioneer species, many desirable woodland plants are able to tolerate a degree of shading through the summer. Without shade these species are at a competitive disadvantage from more aggressive species.

## The impact of disturbance

Disturbance includes harvesting of produce, grazing, cutting, treading, erosion, fire, vandalism and the presence of people and dogs. Compared to most urban and agricultural land uses, woodlands receive a very low intensity of management (in essence, planned disturbance). Irrespective of the quality and diversity of habitats in the woodland, this low intensity of management offers many opportunities for wildlife.

Some types of disturbance are important in maintaining and increasing the wildlife value of woodlands.

- In low-stress environments cutting can reduce the dominance of the few aggressive species that would tend to predominate, and provide opportunities for a greater range of plants. The removal of cut vegetation from the site can be beneficial in removing nutrients and so reducing the competitive advantage of aggressive species.

- Once open ground is colonised it tends to move through a succession of grassland and scrub to colonising woodland, and eventually climax woodland. This succession is not desirable on all parts of a woodland and mowing, flailing and tree felling are ways of arresting the succession to maintain a diversity of habitats in the field, shrub and canopy layers.

- Thinning, group felling or coppicing may be used to maintain shade levels suitable for desirable woodland plants and other woodland floor habitats.

- Light disturbance of the soil and ground vegetation caused by felling and extraction operations provides fresh ground within the woodland for colonisation by pioneer species and can help disperse rhizomes and tubers of species which tend not to spread by seed.
- Controlled grazing is important in wood-pasture and can increase ground flora diversity in some woodland types.

Some types of disturbance reduce the wildlife value of woodlands.

- Urban woodlands are likely to experience high levels of disturbance from site users causing physical damage to vegetation through trampling, vandalism and fire, and disruption to animals with noise and activity.
- Intensive commercial management of woodlands can result in low habitat diversity and hence limited opportunities for wildlife.
- Fragile habitats such as marshy areas and sand banks are very easily damaged, and stressed habitats tend to be slow to recover from damage caused by disturbance.
- Severe disturbance from harvesting and extraction in wet conditions can destroy ground vegetation and encourage colonisation by undesirable species such as heath rush.
- Uncontrolled grazing can be extremely damaging to both woody and herbaceous flora.

## Colonisation and introductions

Species richness can only be increased if new species colonise the woodland. Colonisation will be greatest where there is a nearby pool of desirable species. Woodlands planted adjacent to existing species-rich woodlands or hedgerows will be colonised most quickly by the species they contain if conditions are suitable. There is still much debate about the value of corridors between woodlands for the movement of species. Mobile species such as plants with wind-borne seeds will colonise new woodlands without corridors and immobile species, including many desirable woodland plants, are so slow to colonise that a corridor is unlikely to be of any practical benefit. Corridors may be of benefit to species with dispersal powers between these extremes but species will tend to colonise these areas rather than use them as corridors and so the term linear habitat is probably more meaningful to the understanding of their value.

If increasing ground flora diversity is a high priority in a new woodland with little existing floristic value, the introduction of species commonly found in local woodlands and appropriate to the site type may be considered (Figure 8.1). It is not possible to recreate ancient woodland flora but the introduction of woodland plants can provide food sources for specific invertebrates and can greatly enhance the attractiveness of the woodland. The introduction of ground flora into woodlands has only been undertaken experimentally using container plants (costing between £1200 and £4000 per ha), sowing (costing about £1900 per ha) and introduction of litter and soil from a floristically rich woodland (only undertaken when the source woodland is to be destroyed by development). These techniques are still being evaluated and their success for a range of species monitored.

Success with sowing requires a good seed bed, and weed control prior to planting or sowing has been found to be beneficial in reducing subsequent competition (Figure 8.2). There may be potential for using graminicides to control invasive grasses during the establishment of introductions. Success is generally greatest with infertile substrates where aggressive species are least likely to dominate.

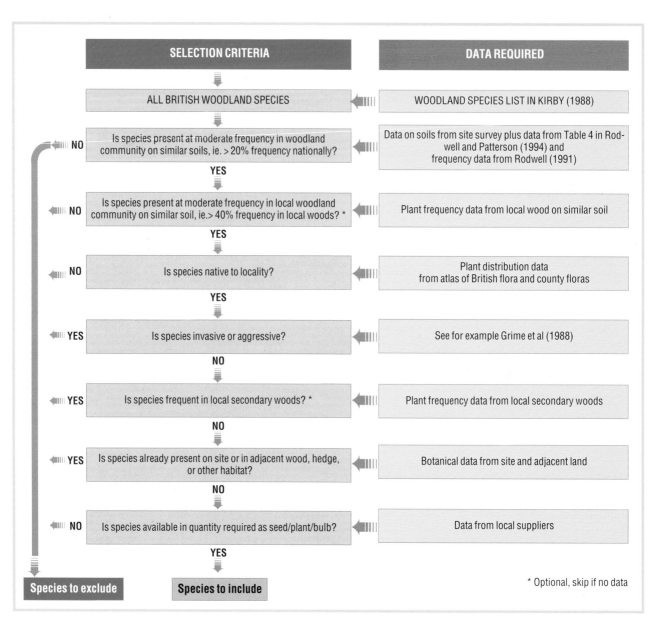

Figure 8.1 The selection of species for introduction of woodland understorey.

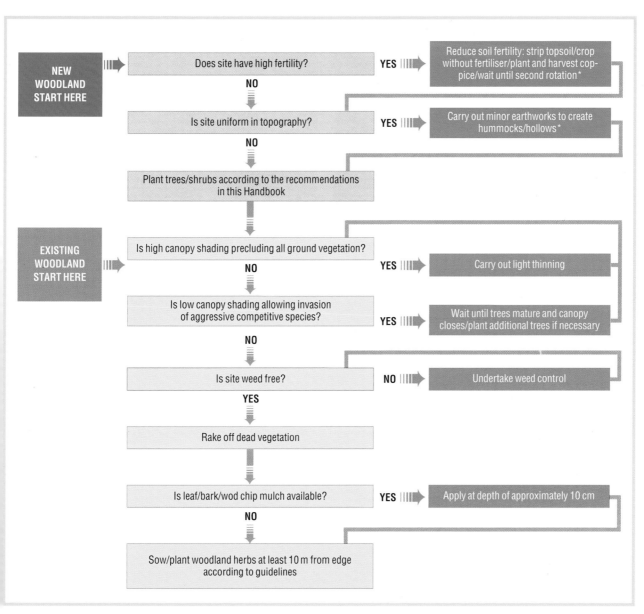

Figure 8.2 Management prior to the introduction of field layer plants into secondary woodland.

Plate 8.10 Wood anemone is a shade tolerant woodland species which is difficult to introduce into new woodlands. Its poor powers of dispersal and exacting site requirements mean that it is largely restricted to ancient semi-natural woodlands. (*40608*)

Plate 8.9 Red campion is a species of woodland edges and hedgerows. Such species tend to be relatively easy to introduce into recently established woodland. (*41099*)

Woodland edge species such as red campion and hedge woundwort can be introduced by sowing into newly planted woodlands or in glades within established woodland, provided that a good seed bed is produced and weed competition is not too intense. Most true woodland species such as primrose and wood anemone tend to establish poorly from seed, and seed is often difficult to obtain so the use of container plants is most likely to be successful. Unless weed control is to be rigorous, the correct level of shading from a tree canopy is needed before planting to prevent the invasion of more aggressive plants (Figure 8.2).

## Choice of tree species

The woody species that are planted or allowed to colonise influence the conservation value and wildlife characteristics of a stand.

- The diversity and species of organisms directly dependent on trees – native species tend to support a greater diversity of flora and fauna than introduced species.

- The availability of physical niches such as holes, standing deadwood and dense foliage – these attributes vary by tree species and include form, evergreen or broadleaf, mature size, longevity and wood durability.

- The shade characteristics at the woodland floor.

- The structure and degradability of leaf litter and its suitability for desirable plants and animals.

- Soil characteristics in the medium and long term.

- The rate of woodland development – the use of species ill suited to the site will result in poor survival, slow growth, and thus delayed achievement of the woodland environment.

Where encouragement of wildlife is a primary objective and site quality allows, the species used should be native to the area and appropriate to the site type. Where it is forthcoming, natural colonisation or regeneration of these species is desirable. Planted stock should be from local seed if the woodland is in the vicinity of long established semi-natural woodlands. Elsewhere, planting stock should be at least of British origin and ideally from similar site types within the native range of the species. Rodwell and Patterson (1994) show the distribution of native woodland types in Britain and advises on species choice, woodland design and silvicultural operations to create new native woodlands with a high conservation potential.

## Stand management for wildlife

Active management of woodland is required to create and maintain a mosaic of habitats and to maintain the right balance of light and shade on the woodland floor (Chapter 7).

Trees become more valuable for nature conservation as they become older and eventually decrepit. For example, many lichens require old bark on which to develop. Moreover, dying and dead wood provides one of the greatest resources for fungal and animal species in the forest. A woodland can lose more than 20 % of its entire fauna if coarse woody debris is eliminated. In general large pieces of

Plate 8.11 This venerable oak is providing a good range of niches for wildlife. (*7863*)

deadwood tend to support a greater diversity of organisms than small pieces, and moist deadwood in shade tends to support a greater diversity of organisms than dry deadwood continually exposed to sunlight.

Native species which are large, long lived and decay slowly, tend to support a greater diversity of organisms than non-native or short-lived trees. Of our native trees, oak is the most important provider of deadwood due to its large size and slow rate of decay. Its prolonged period of old age allows the development of many niches, supporting a diverse fauna. Beech, ash, hornbeam, elm and common lime are some of the other tree species which provide valuable deadwood habitats. Birch, whilst short-lived and rapidly decaying, can create deadwood and rot holes within 70 years (compared with a minimum of 100 years for oak, ash and beech) and supports an important specialist fauna of its own.

Woodland management should aim to provide a range and succession of deadwood habitats, each of which provides particular ecological niches for specialised organisms.

- Dead limbs on living trees.
- Decay columns in trunks and main branches.
- Rot holes in standing trees.
- Standing dead trees.
- Fallen deadwood – trunks and large branches.
- Fallen deadwood – small branches and twigs.
- Stumps and old coppice stools.
- Deadwood in watercourses.

The long-term retention of some mature stands is desirable in most woodlands to provide deadwood habitats. In more intensively managed parts of the woodland, a minimum density of six to eight mature trees, six to eight standing dead trees, and four to five downed trees per ha should be provided where possible. In woodland that is intensively used deadwood on standing trees must not be allowed to become a hazard to visitors (Chapter 2, Urban woodlands and the law). As a rule, trees retained to over-maturity should be well away from paths and heavily used areas.

## Open space management for wildlife

Along with long-term retentions, open space is an important semi-permanent habitat within woodland. In new woodlands careful planning of open space can greatly enhance its potential for wildlife. Between 15 and 20% of open space is usually appropriate and existing areas of diverse ground flora (which are often on the most stressed parts of the site on which it is most difficult to establish trees) should be retained within the open space network, surrounded by a buffer zone if necessary to reduce the extent of future shading (Chapter 4, Site assessment). If the size and shape of the site allows, major conservation rides should have an east–west orientation and a total width not less than the eventual tree height (about 24 m is ideal) to allow sunlight to reach the ground. Sheltered glades on south facing slopes can be a particularly valuable habitat for invertebrates. Even if woodland establishment is to be principally by planting, areas can be left for natural colonisation and succession to take place. It may be appropriate to manage these areas to encourage woody colonisation (Chapter 6).

In established woodlands one of the most important aspects of open space management is the development of a graded woodland edge, from the canopy layer through a shrub and scrambler layer to a rank field layer and possibly to a mown sward. It is also worth creating areas of bare earth as a seed bed for pioneer species.

- **Cutting back and thinning the woodland edge.**
The woodland edge should be cut back as far as required to maintain sunlit conditions in permanent open space. Thinning of the woodland edge on the south and west of glades will also improve sunlight penetration. The woodland edge should not be cut back uniformly; scallops and bays reduce the wind-tunnel effect along rides and further increase the diversity of habitats. In a mature woodland, bays should be at least 25 m long to provide light for a range of plants over an appreciable part of the growing season. Along a ride, opposed bays allow the greatest penetration of light, whilst well-lit glades can be formed by cutting off the corners at ride and path intersections.

Plate 8.12 The most valuable rides for wildlife are wide, sunny and have wide edges grading from the field layer, through a shrub and scrambler zone, into the tree stand.

**The ride management prescription used in Forestry Commission woodlands on sandy soils in east Suffolk**

Within the Sandlings forests, soil-moisture availability limits the rate of vegetation growth, necessitating swiping of the ride every other year only. The centre of the ride (one pass of the swipe) will be cut every other year. Ride margins (at least two passes of the swipe on each side) will be cut every fourth year. Ride margins will be cut alternately so that in one operation the centre of the ride and one margin will be cut. Two years later the centre of the ride and the other margin will be cut. Where ride-side scrub is present beyond the ride margins, this will be flailed every five years, avoiding the cutting of both sides in any one year.

- **Periodic cutting of shrubs and grass sward.**
Without cutting, these habitats are likely to develop into woodland. Management is required to create a varied edge zone, in places grading through the whole spectrum of habitat types, in other places juxtaposing contrasting habitats such as the woodland edge and mown sward. Shrubs should usually be cut on a five- to seven-year cycle, and the rank field layer every two to five years. Annual cutting is needed to encourage short turf species, and ideally cuttings should be removed. Undertake cutting between October and February unless you want to discourage or encourage specific species, in which case cutting should take place at the appropriate growth phase of the target species. Brash from shrub cutting should be removed from the site, or at least

131

Plate 8.13 Woodlands can be valuable for wildlife, amenity and landscape enhancement, and still yield valuable timber. (*40985*)

pulled back under the trees or put into piles 50 m apart.

- **Providing bare ground as a seed bed.** At each cutting cycle a new area of one to two square metres in each bay should be scraped bare of vegetation. Periodic removal of groups of shrubs will also provide bare ground for colonisation.

## Woodlands for timber production

The most profitable woodlands are generally large-scale conifer plantations on fertile sites, managed as high forest and harvested by clear felling. Fast growth minimises the rotation length, the tree species produce straight saleable timber which is relatively cheap to harvest, and the scale and layout of the woodland facilitates cost-effective management, harvesting and extraction. Many urban woodlands will be the antithesis of this but, nonetheless, will still have the potential to yield valuable produce which can go a long way to offset the cost of management for other objectives. Stems of planking-quality hardwood timber can be worth £50 to £60 each standing, the timber value of a woodland containing 120 of these stems per ha being £6000 to £7200 per ha (1993 prices). In most cases it is possible, with sensitive management, for woodlands to yield this level of income without unduly compromising amenity, conservation or landscape objectives. Much of the information in this Section comes from Kerr and Evans (1993).

### Planning for timber production

Future income from timber will be heavily influenced by woodland design and layout so make sure that the potential for timber production is not overlooked at the planning stage. These suggestions should be followed, where site constraints and other objectives allow.

- The scale of planting of any timber-producing species should be large enough to yield saleable parcels from thinning and felling. For high value produce at least one lorry load (30 m$^3$) of timber is usually required to interest a buyer, and for low value pulp wood upwards of 100 m$^3$ is needed.
- The layout of compartments and mixtures should not hinder felling and extraction. Potentially valuable stems can be rendered worthless if the cost of harvesting exceeds timber value.
- Initial spacing of timber-producing species should be close enough to promote the growth of straight stems and encourage early side-branch suppression (Table 8.1).

## Pruning and selective thinning

Soon after the establishment phase formative pruning may be needed in stands of species with low apical dominance, such as oak and beech, and those containing widely spaced trees. The objective of formative pruning is to produce a single straight stem with small branches that will die quickly at the onset of canopy closure leaving the bole knot free. Most conifer species tend to self-prune as the stand develops, but in order to produce high quality broadleaved timber, side branches must continue to be removed before they reach 5 cm diameter. After this size removal becomes difficult and wounds are large enough to be infected by rot fungi. Pruning is usually done in two stages, up to 3 m prior to first thinning and up to 6 m before the second thinning.

Because of the cost of pruning, concentrate effort on potential final crop trees, which is where the greatest timber value lies. Select and mark between 200 and 350 trees per ha (Table 8.2) for pruning and favouring in thinning operations. Some of these trees will be removed in later thinnings but a choice of final crop trees must be maintained. Pruning will also increase the value of those trees that are removed towards the end of the rotation.

## Marketing and utilising timber from urban woodlands

Timber marketing is a neglected discipline, particularly with urban woodlands, and as a result much good quality timber is wasted and much potential income lost. Successful timber marketing requires:

- a sound knowledge of the timber parcel to be sold;

---

**Table 8.1  Recommended minimum stocking at the end of the establishment phase for    production of quality hardwood timber**

| Species | Stems per ha with square spacing (m) |
|---|---|
| Cherry | 1100 |
| Ash | 2500 |
| Sycamore | 2500 |
| Sweet chestnut | 2500 |
| Oak | 3100 |
| Beech | 3100 |

---

### Selecting final crop trees

The selection of final crop trees is best done in winter when the condition of the crown and upper stem can be easily seen. The following criteria, in order of priority, should be used.

1  Good stem form and freedom from defect on the lower 7 m of stem.
2  Absence of deep forking in the crown.
3  Good vigour.
4  Freedom from defect in upper stem and crown, e.g. squirrel damage, evidence of disease.
5  Low incidence of epicormic branching (profuse sprouting from suppressed buds on the tree stem).
6  Proximity of other selected trees – seeking an even spacing of selected trees should only come after the other criteria are satisfied.

**Table 8.2  The number of potential final crop trees to be selected at first thinning, and final crop stocking of the major timber producing broadleaves**

| | Number of potential final crop trees to be selected (stems per ha) and average spacing (m) | Normal final crop stocking (stems per ha) and average spacing (m) | Normal rotation age (years) |
|---|---|---|---|
| Oak | 200 (7.1) | 60–90 (12.9–10.5) | 120–160 |
| Beech | 250 (6.3) | 100–120 (10.0–9.1) | 95–140 |
| Sweet chestnut | 250 (6.3) | 100–190 (10.0–7.3) | 60–70 |
| Cherry | 250 (6.3) | 140–160  (8.5–7.9) | 50–70 |
| Ash | 350 (5.3) | 120–150  (9.2–8.2) | 65–75 |
| Sycamore | 350 (5.3) | 140–170  (8.5–7.7) | 60–70 |

- familiarity with timber markets and how various factors influence price; and
- careful presentation of the timber parcel for sale with provision of accurate supporting documentation for prospective buyers.

The most important aspect of timber marketing is to grow what the market wants. Problems with marketing are usually most acute with low-grade material which has a very limited range of low-value end uses. Markets for softwoods are fairly well developed in Britain and current market prices for different species and products are published in the forestry press. This is not the case for hardwoods and it may be worth using a professional consultant who will be able to:

- grade timber and ensure that the best market prices are obtained: for example, the price differential between second quality and veneer oak can be a factor of 10 and knowing the difference between shake and drying cracks could be critical;
- offer knowledge of the supply patterns from local woodlands, which may allow a cooperative approach to marketing; and
- advise on the best method of sale, point of sale and presentation of timber to potential buyers.

Timber will either be sold standing or felled. Standing sales are relatively easy to organise and minimise the cost to the grower. However, prices will be lower not only because the merchant has to bear the cost of harvesting, but also, with broadleaves, because there remains an element of uncertainty over timber quality. For this reason, high quality hardwoods are usually sold felled to allow inspection for flaws and rot on the cut log ends. Low-grade broadleaves and conifers are generally sold standing.

Plate 8.14  Timber marketing is a neglected discipline which often results in the potential for income from timber not being realised.

Broadleaves should preferably be felled from autumn to early spring, before the sap starts to rise. Ash, beech, sycamore and cherry will start to degrade if left at ride-side for more than six weeks, and so must be sold promptly; oak and sweet chestnut form heartwood and so are much more durable. Conifers can be felled throughout the year as their resin content gives them some resistance to degrade. However, despatch should generally be within six weeks of felling, and within two weeks for pine which is vulnerable to blue-stain fungi.

Much produce from urban woodlands will be of low grade or in small lots. However, with energetic marketing there is great potential in urban areas for finding high-value markets. Niche markets (such as specialist fencing, rustic work, bollards, plant tubs, play equipment, footpath edgings, tree stakes and guards, gates, seats and benches) may be better exploited by converting roundwood into the dimensions required before sale. This can be done through a local saw-mill or with a mobile saw-bench. The proximity of customers offers good market potential for firewood and wood-chips (for footpaths, children's play areas, equestrian surfaces, fuel, compost and mulching).

## Poplars for timber

On large, fertile sites poplars are the most profitable forestry option. Furthermore, woodland can be created quickly, with a canopy height of 6 m after two growing seasons being quite possible.

Plate 8.16 This 21-year-old crop of poplar is approaching harvestable size. (*3905*)

Plate 8.15 With energetic marketing there is great potential in urban areas for finding high value niche markets.

To achieve good growth rates the most productive poplar clones require deep, fertile, freely rootable soils of pH 5.0 to 7.0, with ample and continuous supplies of water, but freedom from waterlogging. For the production of veneer quality timber, two metre sets (Chapter 5, Planting stock quality and type) of an approved clone should be planted at 8.0 × 8.0 m spacing (156 per ha) so that one third of their length is below the surface. Spot weed control for two to three years after planting is critical for the achievement of good early growth rates. Pruning to achieve 6 to 7.5 m of clean stem is needed to attract the premium paid for high quality knot-free timber. Fast growing cultivars on prime sites can reach veneer log size in about 20 years.

Even on poorer quality sites, poplars planted as 25 cm cuttings at 3.0 × 3.0 m spacing can be used for rapid screening and wood production.

## Short rotation coppice

Short rotation coppice is loosely defined as coppice worked on a cycle of less than 10 years. There are several traditional forms of short rotation coppice including hazel for hurdles and thatching spars, sweet chestnut for walking sticks, and osiers for woven baskets. Of more potential in the urban environment is short rotation coppice of poplar and willow. These are easy to establish using 25 cm cuttings (Chapter 5, Planting stock quality and type) and suitable clones are available for most site types. Planting densities of 10 000 per ha for willow and 7000 per ha for poplar are recommended for maximum yield. On the best sites, yields of 10 to 15 dry tonnes per ha per year may be expected with coppicing periods of between two and five years, depending on the harvesting system used and on site and clone productivity.

Plate 8.17   Short rotation coppice using poplars and willows can offer landscape and amenity benefits as well as a high yield of wood-chips. (*40973*)

Nationally, energy production is seen as the principle market for short rotation coppice, but in urban areas the diverse potential uses for wood-chips offer the possibility of breaking the 'no market, no crop: no crop, no market' trap being experienced elsewhere due to the scale of production required for viable energy coppice production. With careful planning poplars and willows can quickly create landscape impact, and provide shelter, screening and a conducive backdrop for recreation and amenity uses. Varying the layout design, choice of clone and cutting cycle offers many opportunities for combining sensitive design with production capability. On difficult sites tough poplars (for example,

137

*Populus alba* 'Racket') and willows (for example, *Salix × dasyclados*) can be used to create a woodland skeleton (Chapter 5, Species mixtures), nursing plots of more sensitive species which will eventually form the character of the woodland. Whilst not as valuable for wildlife as native coppice, short rotation coppice of poplar and willow can be considerably more valuable than intensively farmed agricultural land or urban green-space because of its structural diversity and the relatively low intensity of management.

## For more information

### Publications

Arboricultural Association (1990). *Amenity valuation of trees and woodlands.* Ampfield House, Romsey, Hampshire, SO51 9PA.

Carter, C. I. and Anderson, M. A. (1987). *Enhancement of lowland forest ridesides and roadsides to benefit wild plants and butterflies.* Research Information Note 126. Forestry Commission, Edinburgh.

Countryside Commission (1981). *Informal countryside recreation for disabled people.* Advice Series 15. Countryside Commission, 19–23 Albert Road, Manchester, M19 2EQ.

Chambers, K. (1990). Design issues relating to fear in parks and woodlands. *In: Advice manual for the preparation of a community forest plan.* Countryside Commission, 19–23 Albert Road, Manchester, M19 2EQ.

Department of Transport (1993). The wildflower handbook. *Design manual for roads and bridges. Volume 10, section 4, part 1: HA 67/93.* Head of Highways Policy and Environment Division, DoT, 2 Marsham Street, London, SW1P 3EB.

Douglass, R. W. (1969). *Forest recreation.* Pergamon Press, Oxford.

Ferris-Kaan, R., Lonsdale, D. and Winter, T. (1993). *The conservation management of deadwood in forests.* Research Information Note 241. Forestry Commission, Edinburgh.

*Forestry and British Timber* is a monthly trade magazine that regularly publishes timber auction prices.

Forestry Authority (1992). *Forest recreation guidelines.* HMSO, London.

Forestry Authority (Scotland) (unpublished). *Community woodlands in Scotland: a manual on the presentation of community woodlands.* Portcullis House, 21 India St, Glasgow, G2 4PL. (0141) 248 3931.

Forestry Commission (1989). *Marketing for small woodlands: county lists of mills, merchants and contractors.* Forestry Commission, Edinburgh.

Forestry Commission (1990). *Forest nature conservation guidelines.* HMSO, London.

Forestry Commission (1991). *Community woodland design guidelines.* HMSO, London.

Forestry Commission (1994). *The management of semi-natural woodlands.* Forestry Practice Guides 1 to 8. Forestry Commission, Edinburgh.

*Forests, woodlands and people's preferences.* In preparation, by T. Lee, for the Forestry Commission, Edinburgh.

Francis, J. L. and Morton, A. J. (1992). The establishment of ground flora species in recently planted woodland. *In: Aspects of Applied Biology 29: Vegetation management in forestry, amenity and conservation areas.* Association of Applied Biology, HRI, Wellesbourne, Warwick, CV35 9EF.

Grime, J. P., Hodgson, J. G. and Hunt, R. (1988). *Comparative plant ecology.* Unwin Hyman Ltd, London.

Hibberd, B. G. (1991). *Forestry practice.* Forestry Commission Handbook 6. HMSO, London.

The Institute of Chartered Foresters. *List of members in consultancy practice.* 7A St. Colme Street, Edinburgh, EH3 6AA. (0131) 225 2705.

Jobling, J. (1990). *Poplars for wood production and amenity.* Forestry Commission Bulletin 92. HMSO, London.

Kerr, G. and Evans, J. (1993). *Growing broadleaves for timber.* Forestry Commission Handbook 9. HMSO, London.

Kirby, K. J. (1988). *A woodland survey handbook.* Research and Survey in Nature Conservation 11. Nature Conservancy Council, Peterborough.

Potter, C. J., Nixon, C. J. and Gibbs, J. N. (1990). *The introduction of improved poplar clones from Belgium.* Research Information Note 181. Forestry Commission, Edinburgh.

Ratcliffe, P. R. (1993). *Biodiversity in Britain's forests.* Forestry Commission, Edinburgh.

Richards, G. E. (ed) (1992). *Wood energy and the environment.* Energy Technology Support Unit, DTI, Harwell Laboratories, Oxfordshire, OX11 0RA.

Rodwell, J.S. (ed.) (1991). *British plant communities.* Volume 1: *Woodlands and scrub.* Cambridge University Press.

Rodwell, J. and Patterson, G. (1994). *Creating new native woodlands.* Forestry Commission Bulletin 112. HMSO, London.

Walshe, P. (1990). Designing community forests for the less able. *In: Advice manual for the preparation of a community forest plan.* Countryside Commission, 19–23 Albert Road, Manchester, M19 2EQ.

Willis, F. K. and Benson, J. F. (1989). Recreational value of forests. *Forestry*, **62(6)**, 93–110.

# 9 Freckland Wood: case study of a new woodland

This Chapter is a case study of a new 20 ha woodland on a colliery spoil mound (Plate 9.1) owned by Nottinghamshire County Council and called Freckland Wood. It is being established by Nottinghamshire County Council in conjunction with the Forestry Authority to serve as a demonstration woodland within the Greenwood Community Forest. Although many urban woodlands will be smaller the approach to woodland creation should be the same.

## Getting the ball rolling

The process of woodland creation started with a site meeting between the County Council Forestry Officer and a Forestry Authority urban forester. The objective of the meeting was to discuss the benefits that woodland planting might bring to the site and the locality, and to consider the constraints and opportunities provided by the site. The initial meeting was kept small to enable focused discus-

Plate 9.1 Newstead Tip across Newstead village.

sion of the limitations imposed by the site, the availability of necessary expertise and resources, and the division of responsibilities.

The site was assessed by the County Forestry Officer who was familiar with the chemical and physical characteristics of the substrate, having undertaken schemes on other colliery spoil mounds in the area. Nonetheless, analyses of pH, nitrate nitrogen, phosphorus, potassium, magnesium and conductivity were undertaken to assess the suitability of the substrate as a growing medium. Inspection pits were dug across the site to look at the physical condition of the substrate down through the profile.

The strengths, weaknesses, opportunities and threats inherent in the site were marked on a site plan (Figure 9.1) which provided information to draft the specification.

## Draft specification: the basis for consultation

The draft specification was the basis for initial consultation with interested parties and relevant specialists:

- the Greenwood Community Forest project team (community forest context, public consultation);
- Nottinghamshire County Council officials (authority and finance to proceed);
- Forestry Authority officials (authority and finance to proceed);
- Forestry Authority Woodland Grant Scheme officer (grant aid);
- Nottinghamshire County Council landscape architect and ecologist (design issues and existing wildlife value);

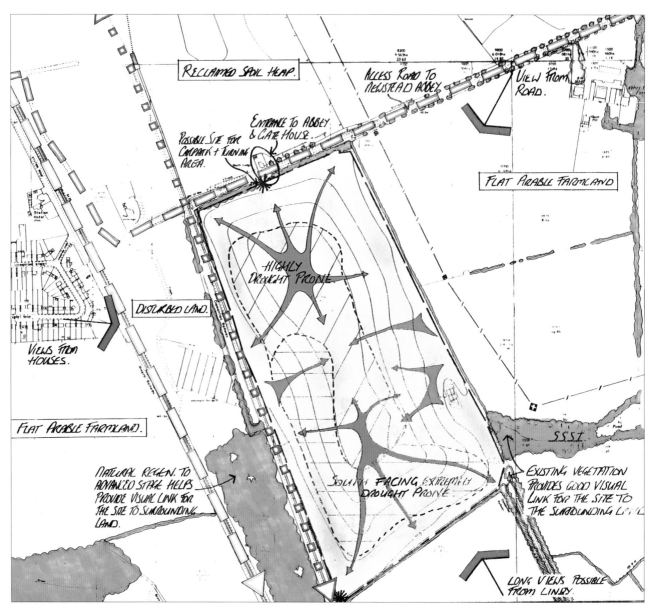

Figure 9.1 By detailing features, strengths, opportunities and potential problems on a site map, a design can be built up around these.

- Forestry Authority wildlife and conservation officer (wildlife potential).

The second draft incorporated recommendations from these parties, after first reconciling their comments with each other and with the silvicultural limitations inherent in the site. The second draft of the specification was then used as the basis for:

- production of the landscape design plan;
- liaison with local residents;
- application for grant aid under the Forestry Authority Woodland Grant Scheme; and
- consultation with the National Rivers Authority and English Nature about a spring and silt pond on site, and an adjacent site of special scientific interest.

## The landscape design plan

Having discussed the design priorities for the site with those involved, a Forestry Authority landscape architect prepared the landscape design for the site (Figure 9.2). Photographs of this prominent site taken from major viewpoints were used to determine how the design would fit into the landscape (Figure 9.3). The principal paths through the site were designed to:

- take people where they want to go;
- give walkers a diversity of experiences on the site; and
- provide a choice of routes.

## Liaison with local residents

A liaison meeting was organised by the Community Link Officer for the Greenwood Community Forest project. Represented at the meeting were:

- Newstead Residents' Association
- Newstead Parish Council
- Newstead School
- local youth and community interests
- coalfield development
- local councillors
- particularly interested residents
- Greenwood project team
- Nottinghamshire County Council Countryside Team
- Gedling Borough Council (planning officer).

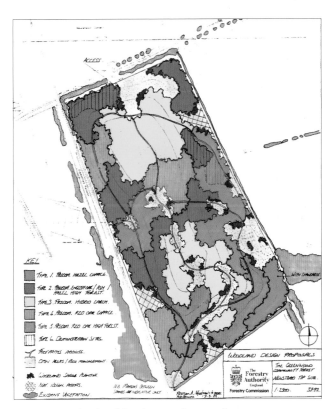

Figure 9.2 The final landscape design plan.

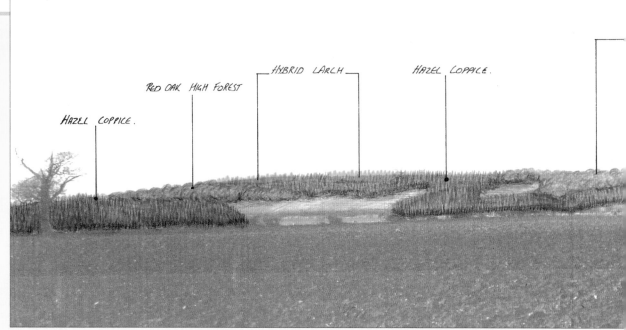

HAZEL COPPICE.    RED OAK HIGH FOREST    HYBRID LARCH    HAZEL COPPICE.

Figure 9.3 Consideration must be given to the impact that a woodland will have in the landscape.
This view of the site from the east is seen from the drive of Newstead Abbey, a popular leisure destination.

144

HAZEL HIGH FOREST.

COPPICE.

HYBRID LARCH.

OAK / ASH / HAZEL HIGH FOREST.

145

Following a very positive initial meeting, where the plan was well received, minor amendments were made to the specification and a series of three further meetings were arranged to discuss the future management and use of the site. A letter was sent to the bodies listed above outlining the form of continuing consultation.

## The final specification

As a result of the second phase of consultation the final specification was produced, including plans for technical demonstration plots to be established in the wood.

Dear

re: **Community Consultation for the Community Forest: Newstead Village/Freckland Wood**

After provisional discussions with various community members in Newstead Village we are now at a stage where some loose but reasonably coordinated 'visions' need to be put on paper as part of the recommendations for community forest creation in this area.

To this end I would like to invite you to take part in a working group which will meet on 3 occasions to put some proposals together for local authorities and landowners to consider. Details of the sessions are enclosed.

At the moment the land available includes the newly planted 'Freckland Wood' (the former south-facing colliery tip) and a strip of land adjacent to this by the railway track.

We acknowledge that villagers will want to talk about other developments in and around the village and hopefully we can do this within the context of the Community Forest.

It must be recognised however that these meetings are a mechanism for putting 'visions' on paper for consideration. No final decisions can be made at this stage, nor can the community forest team make promises to implement all of the visions.

We do promise to:

- listen to your views and ideas;
- advise, as best we can, on the feasibility of these ideas and to make recommendations for their implementation;
- communicate these views to local authorities and landowners as part of the community consultation and involvement process.

It must also be emphasised that these sessions are not meant to be 'public meetings'. They are working group sessions and as such require a relatively small but consistent team attendance.

To ensure that it is a 'task' group rather than a 'discussion' group, I would like to keep the number under 25. A provisional attendee list is enclosed. Apart from those already named there could be room for another 9 residents.

Local people, however, may wish to organise a public meeting to discuss visions amongst themselves and to reach some consensus of ideas. Alternatively, the Newstead Village Newsletter may be an appropriate channel to encourage debate and discussion.

I would be very grateful if you could let me know if you are able to take part in the working group or if you would prefer to send another (named) representative.

I think the meetings will be very positive and creative and will provide a chance for people to speak openly and candidly about their visions and to work together to make this a real Community Forest.

I look forward to hearing from you and thank you for your time.

Yours sincerely

# Specification for urban woodland on Newstead Tip

**Name:**
Freckland Wood

**Project Leaders:**
Martin Glynn for Nottinghamshire County Council
Simon Hodge for the Forestry Authority

**Background:**
The value of demonstrating visually the importance of good silvicultural practice in tree establishment has been shown by the network of 17 demonstration areas throughout the country. With the advent of community forest initiatives on the periphery of the major urban areas of England, new collaborative opportunities have arisen to demonstrate the best and most cost-effective means of establishing urban woodland on often difficult sites.

**Objectives:**
1. To demonstrate to those involved in the community forests the detail and effect of objective based woodland planning, and good silvicultural practice based on recent research results.

2. To gain experience and information on the establishment of trees on Nottinghamshire coal spoils in densely populated areas.

3. To create an attractive woodland with the following hierarchy of objectives:

   a. informal recreation and amenity;

   b. landscape enhancement;

   c. wood production for local utilisation;

   d. enhancement of local wildlife value.

**Site description:**
The site is a distinctive, and obviously man made, mound of 18.8 ha in extent with a NNE/SSW axis. It was a spoil tip from Newstead Colliery which was restored in the early 1970s with only minimal regrading. The tip is about 25 m in height, rectangular in shape and extremely prominent in the landscape (and is a distinct land form on the 1:50 000 OS map). The tip was not capped with topsoil and the substrate into which trees will be planted is a compacted mixture of blue clay and shale.

Substrate chemistry is not a severe constraint to tree establishment on this site. The main problem is severe soil compaction and limited soil moisture availability during the growing season.

| | pH | P mg/l | K mg/l | Mg mg/l | conductivity µ S | nitrate N mg/l |
|---|---|---|---|---|---|---|
| NE quadrant | 6.9 | 3 (0) | 137 (2) | 463 (6) | 2060 (0) | 7 (0) |
| NW quadrant | 6.0 | 5 (0) | 116 (1) | 503 (6) | 2160 (0) | 15 (0) |
| SW quadrant | 6.5 | 3 (0) | 193 (2) | 441 (6) | 2070 (0) | 9 (0) |
| SE quadrant | 7.3 | 3 (0) | 153 (2) | 440 (6) | 2230 (1) | 11 (0) |

*Figures in brackets are ADAS indices.*

*continued*

*continued*

The area is covered by well-established rough grassland which has been grazed until recently. Hedgerows and trees have been successfully established around the periphery of the site about 10 to 15 years ago. A hedgerow planted across the site about 10 years ago is patchy and slow growing. This is likely to be due to lack of weed control as much as inherent site problems.

Within the site, on the NE side, is a spring and a derelict brick silt pond. This feature will be utilised as a silt pond of industrial archaeological interest, or regraded as a more naturalistic pond for conservation and passive recreation.

Although fallow deer are present nearby, they are not likely to be a problem during establishment. Rabbits, hares and voles are likely to be the main damaging pests.

On the east side, the land adjoins farmland and woodland of the Newstead Abbey Estate. To the north is a more recently restored colliery tip. To the west and south is derelict colliery and railway land. The village of Newstead is only 500 m away. Newstead Abbey (owned by Nottinghamshire City Council) is a local tourist attraction and recreational area. The Local Authority intends to fund a light railway along one of the many local derelict railway lines. This will run right by the Newstead Tip site to Mansfield. It is intended mainly for commuter and recreational use. A long distance footpath known as the Robin Hood Way runs nearby, and there is potential for its extension to the Newstead Tip site and beyond to link in with other existing footpath networks.

A large local population will probably make good use of the site. This could lead to problems of vandalism, although it tends not to be a severe problem in this locality.

The land is owned by Nottinghamshire County Council.

The site will be planted according to current recommendations of best practice, in terms of landscape design and conservation value enhancement, as well as silviculture. Various live demonstrations of practical silviculture will be established within the woodland.

### Layout and woodland types:
Pending the results of soil survey and analysis, it is proposed that the 18.8 ha be broadly divided as follows:

| | | | | | |
|---|---|---|---|---|---|
| 1. Predominantly hazel coppice | 3.5 ha | | 5. Predominantly red oak high forest | 1.0 ha |
| 2. Predominantly English oak/ash/hazel high forest | 1.5 ha | | 6. Demonstrations | 1.0 ha |
| 3. Predominantly hybrid larch high forest | 5.0 ha | | 7. Open space | 3.8 ha |
| 4. Predominantly red oak coppice | 3.0 ha | | | |

### 1. Predominantly hazel coppice:
The aim for this area will be to create hazel coppice with 1500 stools/ha. Planting will be with 30% grey alder in group mixture to act as a nurse and a backup. Where hazel establishment is successful, alder will be removed by year 10. This area will provide hazel poles on a 6 to 10 year rotation for hurdles, bean poles, thatching spars, etc. (see Forestry Commission Bulletin 27, *Utilization of hazel coppice*) which would have potential to be marketed locally. Other new or existing areas of hazel in the locality could be organised to create a viable working circle. Planting will be at 1.8 m spacing (3000/ha).

| | | | | | |
|---|---|---|---|---|---|
| 5250 | hazel | 50% | 315 | English oak | 03% |
| 3150 | common alder | 30% | 210 | hawthorn | 02% |
| 1050 | field maple | 10% | 210 | goat willow | 02% |
| 315 | silver birch | 03% | | | |

*continued*

### 2. Predominantly English oak/ash/hazel high forest:

This woodland type corresponds broadly with NVC semi-natural woodland category W8 with pedunculate oak, hazel and ash, which is characteristic of the area. This area will be managed to produce oak and ash high forest. Planting will be at 1.8 m spacing (3000/ha); 30% grey alder in group mixture will act as a nurse and a backup. Where oak/ash/hazel establishment is successful, alder will be removed by year 10.

| 1350 | English oak | 30% | 320 | field maple | 07% |
|------|-------------|-----|-----|-------------|-----|
| 1350 | common alder | 30% | 90 | silver birch | 02% |
| 900 | ash | 20% | 90 | hawthorn | 02% |
| 320 | hazel | 07% | 90 | goat willow | 02% |

### 3. Predominantly hybrid larch high forest:

Hybrid larch for production of valuable rustic poles at thinning and sawlogs at maturity. 30% grey alder in group mixture will act as a nurse and a backup. Where larch establishment is successful, alder will be removed by year 10. Planting will be at 1.8 m spacing (3000/ha).

| 12 000 | hybrid larch | 80% | 750 | silver birch | 05% |
|--------|--------------|-----|-----|--------------|-----|
| 1500 | grey alder | 10% | 750 | aspen | 05% |

### 4. Predominantly red oak coppice:

Predominantly red oak coppice on the poorer soils; 30% grey alder in group mixture will act as a nurse and a backup. Where red oak establishment is successful, alder will be removed by year 10. Red oak is fast growing, produces good quality coppice woodland and is notable for its striking autumn colour.

| 4500 | red oak | 50% | 450 | silver birch | 05% |
|------|---------|-----|-----|--------------|-----|
| 2700 | grey alder | 30% | 270 | rowan | 03% |
| 900 | field maple | 10% | 180 | hawthorn | 02% |

### 5. Predominantly red oak high forest:

Red oak high forest on the poorer soils. This species will be favoured to create the impact that a simple forest structure can have (e.g. mature Chiltern beechwoods). Red oak is fast growing, produces good quality timber and is notable for its striking autumn colour; 30% grey alder in group mixture will act as a nurse and a backup. Where red oak establishment is successful, alder will be removed by year 10.

| 1500 | red oak | 50% | 150 | silver birch | 05% |
|------|---------|-----|-----|--------------|-----|
| 900 | grey alder | 30% | 90 | rowan | 03% |
| 300 | field maple | 10% | 60 | hawthorn | 02% |

### 6. Demonstrations:

There will be three types of demonstration planted within the woodland.

| oak | alder | *Establishment techniques.* 13 × 13 m plots (0.3 ha total) showing the effect of: |
|-----|-------|-----------------------------------------------------------------------------------|
| 150 | 150 | a. Fertiliser/sewage sludge × weed control (fert/weed; fert/no weed; sludge/weed; sludge/no weed; weed; control). Plots of 25 English oak and 25 grey alder at 1.8 × 1.8 m spacing. |

*continued*

*continued*

| | | | |
|---|---|---|---|
| 100 | 100 | b. | Ground preparation × weed control (rip/weed; rip/no weed; no rip/weed; control). Plots of 25 English oak and 25 grey alder at 1.8 × 1.8 m spacing. |
| | | c. | Using different English oak stock types and tree protection (18 275–300 cm standards with stakes at 3.0 × 3.0 m spacing; 33 120–180 cm whips at 2.2 × 2.2 m spacing; 33 40–60 cm undercuts in 1.2 m treeshelters at 2.2 × 2.2 m spacing; 50 40–60 cm undercuts at 1.8 × 1.8 m spacing; 50 40–60 cm cell-grown plants at 1.8 × 1.8 m spacing; direct sowing of acorns at 10 000/ha into rotovated ground [170 acorns in the 13 × 13 m plot], as recommended in Forestry Commission Bulletin 62). |

| | | | |
|---|---|---|---|
| oak | larch | | *Silvicultural systems.* 32 × 32 m plots (0.3 ha total). |
| 110 | | a. | English oak in 1.2 m treeshelters at 3.0 × 3.0 m spacing. |
| 700 | | b. | English oak at 1.2 × 1.2 m spacing. |
| 160 | | c. | Two row English oak, two row European larch at 1.8 m spacing. |

*Objective led community woodlands.* Community woodlands will exist to serve the needs of the community. New types of woodland will have a part to play in fulfilling specific community oriented objectives. 32 × 32 m plots (0.3 ha total).

a. Short rotation coppice using *Salix × dasyclados* and *Populus trichocarpa × deltoides* 'Beaupre' for biomass production and rapid enhancement of land amenity value. Establish at 1.0 × 1.0 m over 70% of the plot area.

b. 'Fruits of the forest' woodland: establishing a woodland for edible fruits and nuts. Overstorey tree species may include walnut, sweet chestnut, black mulberry and wild cherry, which will be at a final stocking of 70/ha. Understorey species may include hazel, blackthorn, damson, elder and crab apple, which will be at a final stocking of 1000/ha. A ground vegetation layer, designed for easy access, would be predominantly blackberry, but may include raspberries, currants and gooseberries.

c. Specialist wood production on difficult sites, e.g. *Laburnum alpinum* and *Robinia pseudoacacia* coppice and *Prunus avium* standards, for production of sought after laburnum turnery wood and valuable cherry stems, as well as a dramatic flowering spectacle in the spring. Planted at 1.8 × 1.8 m spacing; 35% cherry, 25% laburnum, 40% robinia.

## 7. Open space:

Open space will be concentrated, to some extent, on the top of the Newstead Tip to maintain views of the surrounding countryside. Glades and rides will be laid out and managed to maximise the amenity value of the wood as well as its potential for wildlife. The layout of rides should create dispersal corridors for birds, mammals and invertebrates. Most rides should be planned at a width at least equal to the eventual height of the trees. In order to create a more graded edge to rides, where feasible, linear strips of coppice will be established at ride margins. Where possible, irregularly spaced glades and bays, preferably south facing, will be incorporated into the ride system as a means of avoiding a wind-tunnel effect (detrimental to butterflies and other invertebrates) and reducing visual uniformity. The larger unplanted areas will be kept free of ground preparation in order to maintain existing vegetation cover and to help define them during the early establishment phase.

*continued*

*continued*

**Prescription for establishment:**

The basic prescription for the site is:

1. Prepare site with McLarty mounder/wing-tine ripper to a depth of 0.6 m. Ripping oblique to contours.

2. Rabbit fence. Remove or upgrade existing fences where necessary. Erect new fences as required.

3. Notch plant at 1.8 m$^2$ (3000 trees/ha). Use the best quality stock and plant soon after delivery according to an agreed design. Unless otherwise specified, all stock will be 40–80 cm (transplants, undercut or cell grown).

4. Undertake meticulous weed control on 1.0 m$^2$ spots at the base of each tree for 5 years using approved herbicides.

5. Slow release fertiliser in April of second season (and, if necessary, subsequent seasons) according to the needs of the site as indicated by soil analysis.

6. Beat up to planting density at the end of the first and second year and thereafter if plant density falls below 2222/ha.

7. Mow rides and 'fire breaks' as necessary.

**Timing:**

By September end:
    apply sewage sludge to relevant plots
    rabbit fence
    peg out
    rip.

By December end:
    plant
    initial weed with propyzamide.

**Responsibilities:**

Nottinghamshire County Council will:

- prepare draft landscape design proposals;
- undertake and finance necessary soil survey and analysis;
- undertake and finance (through Forestry Commission grants) the laying out, planting and maintenance of the woodland according to the agreed plan of operations;
- finance the materials required for the demonstration plots (as these will be included in the area approved for grant aid);
- undertake an annual beat up survey for the main part of the site.

The Forestry Authority will:

- assist with the preparation of plans and specifications for design and implementation of the scheme, involving Forestry Authority landscape architects and ecologists as necessary;
- organise, lay out, supervise and undertake the establishment and maintenance of demonstration plots for 5 years;
- advise on continued maintenance, management and development of the site;
- assess survival, height and diameter of all demonstration plots annually;
- keep a professional photographic record of the development of the site.

*continued*

*continued*

**Resource requirement:**

40–80 cm (transplants, undercut or cell grown):

| | |
|---|---|
| *Larix × eurolepis* | 12 000 |
| *Quercus rubra* | 6 000 |
| *Corylus avellena* | 5 600 |
| *Alnus incana* | 5 350 |
| *Alnus glutinosa* | 4 500 |
| *Quercus robur* | 2 960 |
| *Acer campestre* | 2 570 |
| *Betula pendula* | 1 760 |
| *Fraxinus excelsior* | 900 |
| *Populus tremula* | 750 |
| *Crataegus monogyna* | 540 |
| *Sorbus aucuparia* | 360 |
| *Salix caprea* | 300 |
| *Laburnum alpinum* | 220 |
| *Prunus avium* | 110 |
| *Prunus spinosa* | 20 |
| *Juglans regia* | 10 |
| *Castanea sativa* | 10 |
| *Morus nigra* | 10 |
| *Sambucus nigra* | 10 |
| *Prunus domestica* | 10 |
| *Malus sylvestris* | 10 |
| *Rubus spp., Ribes spp.* | (numbers to be determined) |

275-300 cm standards (with stakes):

| | |
|---|---|
| *Quercus robur* | 18 |

120-180 cm whips:

| | |
|---|---|
| *Quercus robur* | 33 |

40-60 cm cell grown plants:

| | |
|---|---|
| *Quercus robur* | 50 |

Acorns:

| | |
|---|---|
| *Quercus robur* | 200 |

Rooted cuttings:

| | |
|---|---|
| *Salix x dasyclados* | 400 |
| *Populus trichocarpa x deltoides* 'Beaupré' | 320 |

Rabbit and stock proof fencing; length to be determined.

Wing-tine ripping for 15.0 ha.

Herbicide and fertiliser as necessary.

**Date of review meeting for preparation of first management plan:**  May 1998.

**Location:**  Newstead, Nottinghamshire.  SK527 525.

**Written by:**  S. Hodge 10/02/92.

**Approved by:**  Principal Silviculturist (for the Forestry Authority).
Head of Planning and Economic Development (for Nottinghamshire County Council).

**Distribution:**  Forestry Authority (England) office
Countryside Commission
Nottinghamshire County Council (Planning and Economic Development)
Greenwood Community Forest
Forestry Authority Forester

## Implementation

There were several parties involved with implementation and clear and regular communication was essential to translate the specification and design into woodland on the ground.

- Nottinghamshire County Council – preparation of the tree planting and maintenance contract; initial grass cutting over the whole site; application of phosphate over the whole site; organisation of the ground preparation contract.
- The Forestry Authority – establishment and maintenance of one hectare of demonstrations; specialists at the University of Central England's School of Landscape helped to create the 'fruits of the forest' area.
- Contractors – a contract for ground preparation and a more complex contract for the planting and early maintenance of the scheme were let.

## The tree establishment contract

The tree establishment contract was prepared on the basis of the specification and landscape design, and was let by multiple tender well before the deadlines for commencement of work. Site meetings were held to ensure that instructions and arrangements were understood. Regular liaison took place during the ground preparation, laying out and planting operations. Implementation of the layout was aided by marker posts put on site at the location of grid intersects on the site plan. The main contract covered planting and early maintenance ensuring that any initial losses are replaced at the contractor's expense.

Plate 9.2 a & b  A contract was let for a combined ripping/mounding operation to provide suitable planting positions.

## Conditions of contract for the establishment of woodland on Newstead Tip

### Work section 1: Plants and plant handling

GENERAL: Planting shall be carried out in such a manner as to ensure that the plants can establish and develop successfully.

SUPPLY OF PLANTS: Plants shall be supplied from the nurseries listed. The nursery(ies) shall be informed that the stock is required for Nottinghamshire County Council Department of Planning and Economic Development.

QUALITY OF PLANTS: All plants shall meet the Specification and BS 3936 Part 1 Nursery Stock and Part 4 Forest Transplants and be certified British grown.

INSPECTION OF PLANTS: The Contractor shall notify the Supervising Officer of the numbers, species and sizes of plants to be supplied from each nursery at least two weeks before planting operations are to start. The Contractor shall, when requested, make arrangements for the Supervising Officer to inspect the plants at the nurseries before, during or after lifting for approval before dispatch.

BUNDLING: Bundles of bare-rooted plants shall consist of graded plants of one species with all shoots facing the same direction. Bundles shall contain equal numbers of plants. Any part bundles shall be clearly marked. Bundles shall be tied securely with supple material which will not, by its nature or tension, cause damage to the plants.

LABELLING: Each individual or plant bundle, bag or lot of one species of plants shall be labelled by the supplier with a securely attached durable printed label. The PLANT NAME, SIZE and QUANTITY in the bundle or bag, and the TOTAL QUANTITY in the consignment shall be clearly and durably displayed on the label together with the SUPPLIER'S NAME. Forestry species specified under the EEC Forest Reproductive Materials Regulations (1977) shall be labelled in accordance with those Regulations.

PACKAGING: Bare-root plants shall be entirely enclosed in plastic film bags (250 gauge minimum) securely tied at the top. Plants shall be loosely bundled within the bag, which shall be of an adequate size. All shoots must face in the same direction so that roots and shoots are not in contact. Container-grown plants will not normally receive additional packaging, but degradable pots shall be enclosed in polythene film (minimum 250 mm gauge) and firmly secured, as will cell-grown plants not supplied in the cell.

TRANSPORT: On open lorries, all plants shall be loaded, stacked and unloaded in such a way that breakage or crushing by the weight of plants above, or the security ropes will not occur. The consignment shall be completely and firmly covered with opaque sheeting in such a way that there is the minimum draught under the sheet from the direction of travel. Plants in polythene bags shall be sheeted so that they are shaded from direct sunlight. In closed lorries or containers, all plant material shall be loaded in such a way that breakage or crushing by the weight of plants above is avoided during loading, transit and unloading. Where transport is entrusted to others, not under the control of the supplier or the purchaser, consignments shall be clearly addressed, in manageable units, securely crated or packaged to withstand mechanical damage.

HANDLING OF PLANTS: The Contractor shall ensure that plant handling complies with the 'Recommendations for Plant Handling – from Lifting until Delivery to Site' in *Plant handling* published by the Committee for Plant Supply and Establishment 1985. The Contractor shall give the Supervising Officer at least 2 working days notice before planting so that each batch of plants can be inspected before use. Handle plants carefully to reduce as far as possible injury by mechanical shock and crushing.

*continued*

*continued*

## Work section 2: Planting

SITE PREPARATION: All rubbish and debris shall be removed from site to tip.

SETTING OUT: Each compartment shall be marked out with clearly visible markers at 10 m intervals and every change of direction for approval by the Supervising Officer. The markers shall be removed on completion of the planting.

PLANTING SEASON: All planting is to be completed by 31 December 1992. Subsequent beating up shall be completed by 1 February of the relevant year.

PLANTING CONDITIONS: Planting shall only be carried out in suitable conditions avoiding periods when the site is waterlogged, when snow is lying or when the ground is frozen. When there is a frosted crust no deeper than 25 mm this may be screefed off and shall then be broken up and disposed of by distribution around each pit.

PLANT SPACING: All plants shall be planted at 1.8 m × 1.8 m spacings.

PLANTING PATTERN: This shall be groups of at least 9 and no more than 16 of each species evenly spaced throughout the plot, unless otherwise shown on the drawings.

FORMATIVE PRUNING: All containers and non-degradable wrapping shall be removed immediately prior to planting. Dead and damaged roots and stems shall be cut back cleanly to the nearest growth point. Additional pruning shall be carried out to ensure the plant has a well balanced form typical of the species. Where appropriate the plant shall have a dominant central leading shoot. Plants with major damage shall be rejected.

PLANTING: Plants shall be planted vertically into a L or T notch to the depth of the root collar. The roots shall be well spread and firmed after planting. The exact planting position relative to the mound/rip line will be determined on site once ripping is completed. The roots of bare-rooted plants shall be evenly spread. Container medium shall be lightly disturbed and any tightly matted roots teased out.

## Work section 3: Fencing

RABBIT FENCING: The site has been previously rabbit fenced. This shall be inspected by the contractor and, prior to planting, upgraded to his satisfaction to ensure total exclusion of rabbits.

RABBIT PROOF GATE: Prior to planting a rabbit proof gate will be erected at the main site entrance, to drawing No. ___. Additional permanent fencing (to the same standard as existing fencing) shall be erected between the gateposts and existing fence strainers as necessary.

STILES: Stiles to drawing No. ___ will be erected at the points indicated by the Supervising Officer. These shall be permanently rabbit proofed.

RABBIT CONTROL: The contractor shall undertake a humane rabbit control programme, the details of which shall be agreed with the supervising office, before any planting works on the site commence.

N.B. In the event of non-compliance with any of the above clauses, the contractor shall be held responsible for all rabbit damage to plant material.

## Work section 4: Establishment maintenance of forestry areas

MAINTENANCE - GENERAL: The Contractor shall maintain all areas of work during the 30 months following practical completion. A programme of maintenance visits shall be agreed with the Supervising Officer at the commencement of the maintenance period. Failure to do this may result in non-payment for works undertaken. The Supervising Officer will require prior notification of each maintenance visit to the site. Failure to give this notification may result in non-payment to the Contractor for any items claimed to have been carried out.

*continued*

*continued*

LEAFING OUT INSPECTION: The Supervising Officer will carry out a leafing out inspection during June. Plant material which has not leafed out shall be replaced by the Contractor entirely at his own cost, during the plant replacement operations. The Supervising Officer shall notify the Contractor in writing of the extent of plant losses at the leafing out stage.

HERBICIDE TREATMENTS - GENERAL: Chemicals and products subject to the provisions of the Poisons Act 1972, Poisons List Order 1982 and the Poison Rules 1982 shall only be used with approval from the Supervising Officer. The use of chemicals marketed in the UK which are included in the Priority Red List at any time during the duration of the contract, are not permitted to be used within the contract. Comply with the Approved Code of Practice: The Safe Use of Pesticides for Non-Agricultural Purposes. HSE, HMSO (1991). Observe sections I and II of Draft Code of Good Agricultural Practice for the Protection of Water. MAFF, HMSO (1991). The Supervising Officer will require the necessary proof of training of all pesticide operators/users, and the appropriate Certificates shall be presented to the Supervising Officer at the commencement of the Contract Period.

WEED CONTROL: From the 31 March following initial planting, establish and maintain a 90% vegetation free ring 1000 mm diameter centred on each plant or the entire area of mulch for the duration of the contract period. The herbicide(s) and method of application shall be approved by the Supervising Officer before work starts.

CONTROL OF NOXIOUS WEEDS: All injurious weeds as defined by the Weeds Act 1959 plus mugwort and other noxious weeds as directed by the Supervising Officer shall be cut/sprayed before seeding commences. The herbicide, method and timing of application shall be agreed with the Supervising Officer before work starts.

GENERAL GRASS CUTTING: Grass cutting shall be carried out when ground and weather conditions are favourable. All grass shall be effectively mown to a height of 100 mm.

FERTILISING: During April of the second growing season apply fertiliser, of a formulation and at a rate agreed with the Supervising Officer, around each tree.

REMOVAL OF LITTER: During each maintenance visit to the site all litter which has accumulated on the site shall be picked up and removed off site to tip.

PRUNING: During each maintenance visit to the site all plant material shall be inspected and checked for damage to branches, shoots and/or bark. All dead and/or damaged branches/shoots and epicormic growth shall be cleanly cut back to sound undamaged wood, using secateurs or pruning saws as appropriate. The wounds to bark shall have the ragged ends trimmed using a sharp knife. In the case of shrub material, deadwood and suckers shall be removed at the base of the plant, unless otherwise directed. The Contractor shall allow in his rates for the cutting back of oversized plant material or certain types of shrubs in early spring, to encourage bushiness. All prunings/trimmings shall be removed off site to tip.

PLANT REPLACEMENTS: The Supervising Officer will inspect the site during September/October, to determine the nature and extent of plant losses. The information collected at the earlier leafing out inspection will also be taken into account. The replacement of plant material which has failed or been badly damaged by herbicide application and which is, in the Supervising Officers opinion, the Contractor's responsibility shall be replaced by the Contractor entirely at his own expense. The replacement of plant material which has failed and which is, in the Supervising Officer's opinion, not the Contractor's responsibility (eg vandalism), shall be replaced by the Employer, expenditure being covered by the Provisional Sum in the Schedules. Failure due to weather conditions will only be covered by this clause if, in the opinion of the Supervising Officer, these conditions are of an extreme nature not foreseeable. The Contractor's rates for all replacements will be based upon the rate for supplying new stock specified. The replacement planting will be carried out in November/December, and prior to the work commencing the Contractor will have received written instruction from the Supervising Officer stating those replacements the Contractor is deemed to replace and those for which additional payment will be made, as specified above.

*continued*

*continued*

FIRMING: All plants shall be regularly inspected and firmed in and kept vertical as required.

INSPECTION AND MAINTENANCE OF GUARDS AND FENCING: Fencing will be regularly inspected and repaired as necessary to the standard as specified. Any items that need to be replaced which are not defective items originally supplied shall be instructed by the Supervising Officer, and shall be paid for out of a provisional sum included in the Schedules.

**Work section 5: Handover**

HANDOVER - GENERAL: Upon satisfactory completion of all construction and planting works the Supervising Officer shall issue the Certificate of Practical Completion. Upon satisfactory completion of all works, including establishment maintenance works, the site/completed areas may be considered for handover. The final Certificate will be issued provided the following conditions apply.

CONDITIONS FOR HANDOVER: The site/areas of the site will be accepted for handover upon the following conditions:

a. All work is of the standard specified.
b. A final stocking assessment has taken place.
c. Establishment maintenance works have been satisfactory.
d. Any defective work, including any settlement has been made good.
e. Plant losses have been rectified according to the Conditions of Contract and replacements planted.
f. Compounds and all temporary works have been removed.
g. The site and boundaries to the site are in a clean, weed free and tidy condition.

# Promotion and interpretation

Local media were regularly updated on plans and progress and an interview about community involvement in the project was broadcast on Radio Nottingham. The community and schools arranged tree planting events during the planting season, involving local people on the ground and encouraging their continuing interest in the site (Plate 9.3). The site is used by the community forest team as a demonstration, a venue, and an example of the wider vision for the community forest.

On-site interpretation has been provided to give information on site history, objectives for the woodland, site features, and demonstration areas.

Plate 9.3 Community tree planting helps to increase the extent to which Newstead villagers feel a sense of ownership of the scheme.

Plate 9.4   The main lectern sign at the principal access point to the site. (*40986*)

A three-tier system of signs was used (Plates 9.4, 9.5 and 9.6), based on designs developed by the Forestry Commission's Public Information Division.

   A Countryside Commission grant covered the cost of woodwork and three copies of the screen printed signs. With screen printing, production of additional copies is relatively inexpensive and is advisable if vandalism is likely to be a problem.

Plate 9.5   Secondary milepost signs interpret demonstration areas and points of interest. (*40988*)

Plate 9.6   Fencepost signs explain individual treatments within the demonstration areas. (*40987*)

# For more information

## Publications

Hodge, S. J. (1993). *Setting up tree planting and woodland demonstrations.* Research Information Note 242. Forestry Commission, Edinburgh.

Forestry Authority (Scotland) (unpublished). *Community woodlands in Scotland: a manual on the presentation of community woodlands.* Portcullis House, 21 India St, Glasgow, G2 4PL. (0141) 248 3931.

## Advice

The Forestry and Land Management Team, Planning and Economic Development, Nottinghamshire County Council, Trent Bridge House, Fox Road, West Bridgford, Nottingham, NG2 6BJ.

# 10 Belvoir Park Forest: case study of an existing woodland

Just as the establishment of new urban woodlands needs to be guided by clear, objective led specification and design (Chapter 4, Drafting a specification), so too does the management of existing woodland, particularly if the woodland supports a variety of uses. A five-year plan should be drawn up at the end of the establishment phase and this plan should be formally reviewed and updated at the end of each period (Chapter 7, Silvicultural management of recently established woodland). This Chapter describes the management of Belvoir Park Forest, indicating the range of issues that are covered in the management plan, and outlining practical aspects of the management of this multi-purpose, urban fringe woodland.

Belvoir Park Forest is a 75 ha woodland on the Southern outskirts of Belfast (Figure 10.1) which attracts an estimated 300 000 visits per year. Planting began in 1961, building on the parkland of the original Belvoir Park Estate. It is owned by the Department of Agriculture for Northern Ireland and managed by the Department's Forest Service.

Despite such intensive use, large parts of Belvoir Park Forest are successfully managed for timber production. The potential of the Forest as a recreation, landscape, wildlife and timber resource is being carefully developed by planning and appropriate woodland management. Whilst the woodland managers freely admit they still have much to learn, their approach will ensure that Belvoir Park Forest yields its range of benefits in a sustainable way.

## The woodland

Belvoir Park Forest (Figure 10.2) comprises 12 ha of mature predominantly broadleaved woodland, 5 ha of younger broadleaved woodland (principally oak and grey alder) and 47 ha of predominantly coniferous woodland planted between 1961 and 1981 (principally Scots pine, Japanese larch, Lawson cypress and Norway spruce; (Plate 10.1). The retention of broadleaved trees on the woodland edge along rides and paths (both from the original Belvoir Park, and from natural regeneration) gives a character of mixed woodland even in the conifer compartments (Plate 10.2).

Within the wood is 11 ha of open space which includes an area of parkland with scattered specimen trees, a 4 ha open space for events, car parking and a small camp site. Three historical features add further interest: an Anglo-Norman motte; an ice house dating from the 1740s; and a graveyard possibly dating back to Norman times. Remnants of the ornamental tree planting in the estate gardens remain and fish ponds from the same period are being restored. The western boundary of the wood is formed by the River Lagan and two streams run through the wood into the river. The long south-eastern boundary of the wood abuts the housing estates and playing fields of the Belfast suburb of Newtownbreda (Plate 10.3). The Forest is an important access route to the city for water, sewerage and electricity services.

Plate 10.1  The main entrance of Belvoir Park Forest through a formal, predominantly coniferous area.

Plate 10.2  Glades and scattered mature broadleaves give the feel of mixed woodland even where conifers predominate.

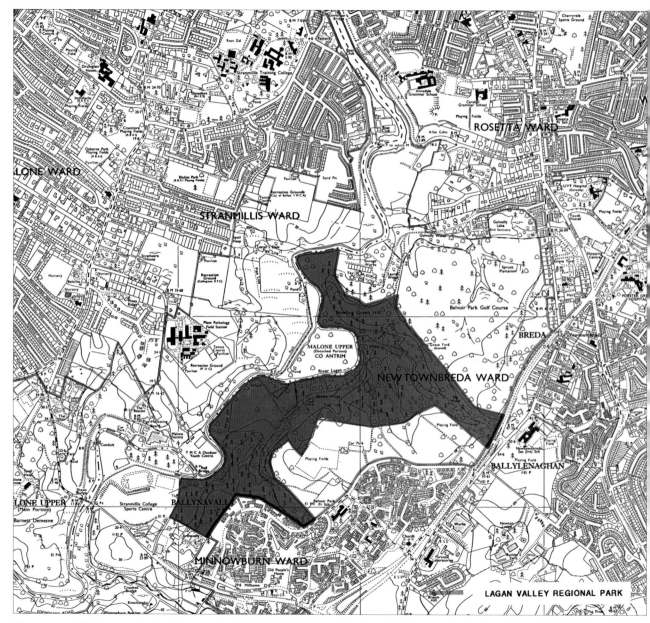

Figure 10.1 The location of Belvoir Park Forest.

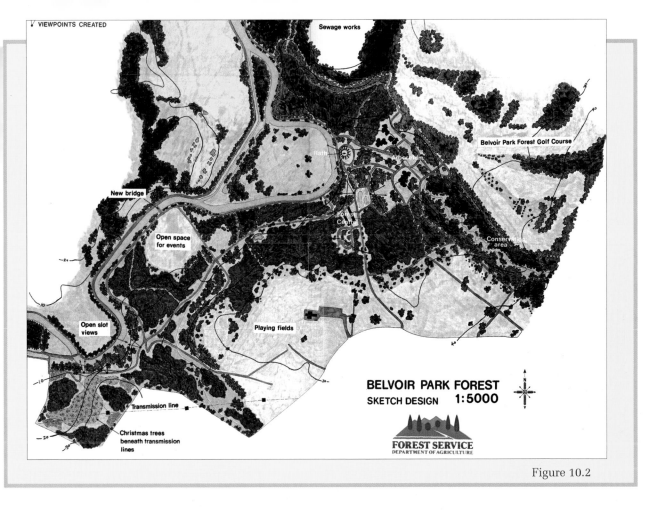

Figure 10.2

## The regional context

Belfast is a city of 500 000 people largely contained within the valley of the River Lagan (Figure 10.1). The Lagan Valley Regional Park is a green wedge that penetrates to the heart of the city, and Belvoir Park Forest is the only major woodland within the Park. At another level, Belvoir and the Lagan Valley are important to the vision of the 'Forest of Belfast', an initiative for environmental improvement and education in the city. Consultation and coordination have ensured that the management directions for the Forest are supporting the objectives of these wider initiatives. The commitment to communication is made clear in the management plan and this is manifest in liaison over particular projects such as plans for pond creation and improved footpath links along the Lagan Valley.

163

The prominence of Belvoir Park in the landscape is hinted at by the name, which means 'beautiful view'. The woodland can be seen from many parts of the city and from hills on the north-west edge of the city. Although the woodland is not yet mature its landscape contribution is already significant. When felling is required landscape impact will be a major consideration and plans have been made to accommodate this.

## Recreation, amenity and woodland users

A survey carried out during 1992/93 recorded 33 500 vehicles entering the forest. Allowing for the large number of visitors on foot from the extensive residential areas on the southern edge of the woodland and through the footpath network of the Lagan Valley Regional Park, it has been estimated that there are about 300 000 visits to the Forest each year. The accessibility of the woodland is further enhanced by a special recreational Ulster Bus service, the 'Lagan Valley Pony', which connects different parts of the Lagan Valley with the main city bus routes. A small, informal campsite within the Forest is used mainly by visitors to Northern Ireland.

The Forest is used principally for walking, dog walking, jogging, picnicking and bird watching. The Forest Service allows organised barbecues including small family barbecues which are becoming increasingly popular. There are 90 car parking spaces, picnic tables and several way-marked routes. Routes are colour coded and clearly displayed on interpretative panels in the parking area and at main access points to the wood (Plate 10.4). Several leaflets are available which describe the history of Belvoir Park and points of information and interest in the woodland. Visitors are kept informed of thinning and other major operations through strategically placed notices that explain what is happening and why. One of the major open spaces within the Forest is used for events and for a recent event a sculpture, telling the story of the area, was created from locally grown ash to add a focus in this open area (Plate 10.5).

The network of paths within the Forest has been developed to accommodate the high intensity of use. By routing a path around much of the eastern boundary, the maximum length of walk is offered with a rich variety of views both into and out of the woodland. Other paths in the eastern half offer shortened routes that make the most of historical, water and landscape features. The western half has

Plate 10.5 A sculpture, created for a recent event, adds interest to a large open space.

a lower intensity of paths and gives more opportunity to enjoy peace and tranquillity. Where possible way-marked routes and roads used during forestry operations are kept separate.

There is a policy of removing dense undergrowth adjacent to paths to improve the sense of personal security. Way-marked routes are regularly inspected for safety, and hazards, such as dangerous trees or erosion to paths, dealt with. The river valley provides ideal conditions for the caustic giant hogweed. Notices warn visitors to avoid, and alert staff to, this plant which is removed when found.

Each year about 3500 school children visit the wood and part time guides are employed to maximise the educational value of the visit. An old stable building has been converted into a forest classroom.

Plate 10.4 Interpretative panels show waymarked routes within the wood.

Considering the large number of visitors to the wood, conflicts between the various site uses are few and arise mainly from dog fouling and unauthorised cross-country cycling which disturbs walkers and is causing erosion to the motte. The amount of intentional vandalism and antisocial behaviour in the wood is low and manageable. The main vehicular access to the wood is closed each day before sunset which must contribute to the low occurrence of rubbish dumping and other antisocial activities.

Visitors to the woodland and those living in the neighbourhood appear to accept the concept of a working woodland, and understand that thinning and felling operations do not threaten the woodland, but are part of the management cycle necessary to improve and perpetuate it. This is partly because the woodland has always been managed on silvicultural principles and partly because of the efforts of the Forest Service to inform woodland users about woodland management operations.

District Conservation Committees, which have existed since the 1970s, formalise consultation between the Forest Service and the voluntary and statutory conservation organisations, and have also fostered the development of good working relationships on an informal basis.

The involvement of local people in the management of the Forest is still in a relatively early stage of development and is currently somewhere between information and consultation on the ladder of participation (Chapter 3, The nature of community involvement). The conscious consideration of community participation started in 1992 when local people formed The Friends of Belvoir Park in response to a threat to part of the wood from a proposed motorway. The group now has over 1000 members who are actively interested in the management of the woodland. The Forest Service encourages the interest of the Friends, and members are

kept informed of operations, such as thinning, which are to take place. The positive nature of this relationship is naturally increasing the amount of feedback from, and consultation with, members over the management of the woodlands. The ladder of participation is being climbed, not in a contrived way, but as a natural consequence of the developing relationship between woodland managers and local people.

## Wildlife conservation

The woodland is recognised as an important wildlife resource both for its own value and for the amenity value of wildlife. Management operations will further increase wildlife value and diversity, and an 8.5 ha block which has been broadleaved woodland since at least 1834 has been designated as a forest nature reserve. Access to this part of the wood is not encouraged in order to keep levels of disturbance to a minimum.

## Timber production and resources for woodland management

Belvoir Park Forest is managed with five other woodlands in the area by a forester and five operatives. In addition, a part-time caretaker and forest guides, available on a call out basis, help with the recreation and education work load. The equipment used in forest management consists of a tractor, dump truck, flail mower, chainsaws, clearing saws and hand tools.

Currently the only timber production is from first thinning of conifer crops, which is undertaken according to the standard forest management yield tables (Forestry Commission Booklet 34). Current production is about 200 m$^3$ per year and over the next decade a steadily increasing thinning programme will yield an average income of £2500 per year (1993 prices). From 2005 onwards the harvesting programme will include 0.5 ha per year of clearfelling and will yield an income in the region of £10 000 per year. The felling programme is designed to spread the age class distribution within the woodland to further landscape, amenity and conservation objectives.

The urban location of Belvoir Park Forest is used as an opportunity for the sale of Christmas trees. About 7000 trees are sold annually, yielding a margin of £10 000 over the total cost of growing, cutting, transporting and retailing the trees. Irrespective of the income generation potential of this enterprise, it is considered worth while for the promotion of the Forest.

Whilst the woodland is not a commercial proposition, income derived from sale of timber and Christmas trees is important in offsetting some of the cost of management.

## Management planning

For Belvoir Park Forest to accommodate the range and intensity of activity that it does, careful planning of management operations is required, to minimise incompatibility between uses and to maintain the capacity of the woodland to serve as a multipurpose resource in the future. The management objectives for the Forest are broadly prioritised.

1. Recreation and amenity

2. Landscape enhancement

3. Wildlife conservation

4. Timber production

Given these overall objectives, a form of informal zoning has developed in the Forest (Figure 10.3) with a recreation emphasis around the main access and by the River Lagan, a conservation emphasis in the forest nature reserve, and a greater emphasis on timber production within the main conifer blocks.

The management of the Forest is directed by a management plan which is updated every five years and contains:

- legal summary
- summary of management directions
- recreation and landscape development plan
- forest nature reserve management plan
- plan of forestry operations.

The management plan is kept as concise as possible and only gives details of operations where there is a need to modify standard silvicultural practice in the light of recreation, landscape or conservation objectives. As much information as possible is presented on clear, uncluttered maps, some of which indicate the present state of the woodland (legal aspects, land use, potential hazards to safe working, road categories and fire plan, features of recreation and conservation importance, and landscape analysis) and others which indicate the programme of work (thinning, felling, and planned management to improve amenity and landscape value).

### The legal summary

The legal summary contains written and mapped information covering:

- ownership and details of leases
- reserved rights (roads, minerals, shooting, fishing, etc.)
- boundary obligations and agreements
- rights of way

- wayleaves and utilities (telephone, electricity, water, etc.)
- restrictions on planting
- archaeological designations
- conservation and landscape designations.

## The summary of management directions

The summary gives an overview of management objectives and an indication of required non-standard and site-specific management operations. It is supported by maps, a statement of the strategic

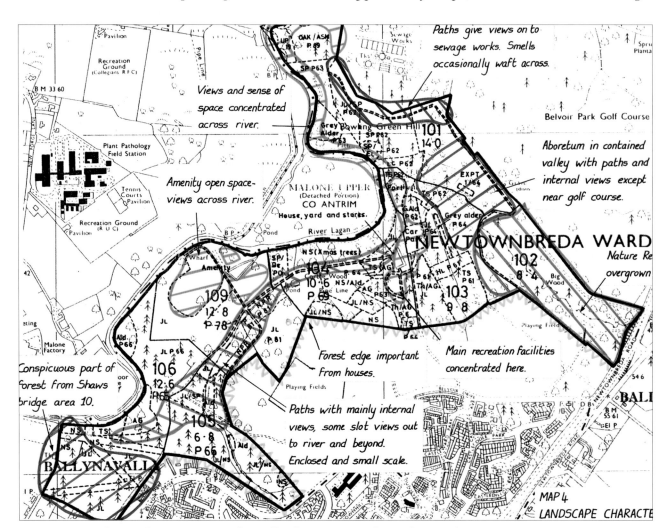

Figure 10.3 Landscape character areas and woodland use zones within Belvoir Park Forest.

value of the woodland, and an annual budget outline.

## The recreation and landscape development plan

In the light of the importance of Belvoir Park Forest as an amenity, recreation and landscape resource, a forest design consultant was used to give recommendations on how to realise the potential of the woodland. The main objective of this exercise was to improve and protect the landscape contribution of the woodland and to create a better environment for informal recreation. A secondary objective was to provide an improved recreation infrastructure within the landscape framework.

Areas of distinct landscape character were identified and characterised (Figure 10.3). There is a general pattern of greater organisation and formality of landscape and use at the hub of the woodland around the car park and education centre, and a gradual reduction in formality and management intensity deeper into the forest and further away from the hub. This trend has influenced the management prescriptions for the various parts of the woodland. Woodland design prescriptions are summarised on one map (Figure 10.4) but specific

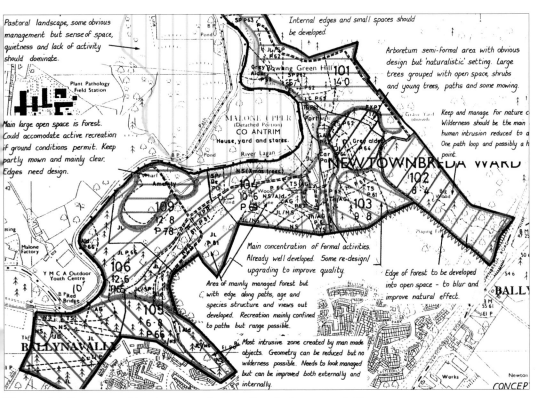

Figure 10.4 Summary of landscape and recreation design prescriptions.

recommendations are detailed for the units defined by the landscape character map.

The recommendations for the south-west part of the Forest serve as a good example of the level of prescription appropriate to this woodland. Power-line wayleaves have resulted in a series of straight parallel edged spaces running zigzag fashion through this area. The resulting geometric layout and shapes affect internal views in this part of the wood, but also mar the prominent views from an adjacent road and a Lagan Valley Regional Park car park. The feature is further exaggerated by the contrast between the larch either side of the wayleaves and the Christmas trees (Norway spruce) planted under the power-lines. The design solution (Figure 10.5) is to fell much of the larch (there is a good market for small dimension larch in urban areas for larch-lap fencing and garden woodwork) and replant with Christmas trees and broadleaves to break up the regular geometry and minimise the impact of the wayleaves on the sky line.

## The forest nature reserve management plan

This plan describes the forest nature reserve, indicating strengths, weaknesses, opportunities and threats. Management objectives for the five-year plan are then defined.

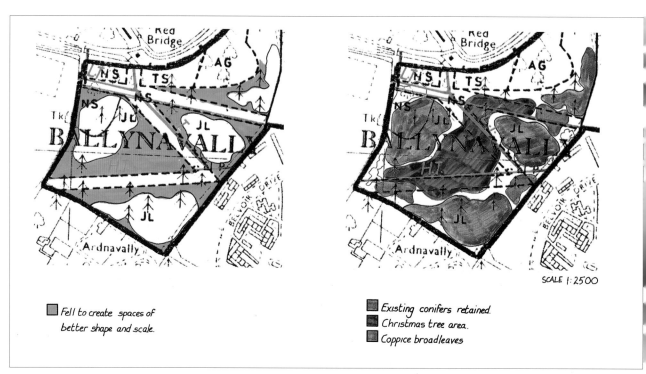

Figure 10.5 Design prescription for a prominent part of the Forest affected by power-lines.

- Improve habitat diversity.
- Increase educational usage.
- Curtail spread of invasive species.
- Initiate research into bird and invertebrate populations.

Management prescriptions for the five-year period are clear and concise.

Improve access to the reserve by upgrading existing path along the north-east boundary. Extend the path across the stream to emerge from the reserve via the old stone lane on the southern boundary.

- Commence clearance of laurel, rhododendron and sycamore at the northern reserve edge.
- Improve structural diversity by clearing five open spaces each of 0.2 ha in the next five years, particularly utilising areas containing dead elm and invasive species clearance. Deadwood should be left on site.
- Recolonisation of these clearings by sycamore should be prevented. The most practical method of regeneration will be the planting of stock grown from locally collected seed. A school class should be encouraged to adopt each clearing and become involved in seed collection, tree growing, planting and tending, as well as ecological studies of the clearing.
- Open up short sections of the stream commencing at the down-stream end. The amalgamation of open space along the stream with some of the clearings would be beneficial.

## The plan of forestry operations

A plan of forestry operations for the five-year period are presented in tabular (Table 10.1) and map forms. The plan indicates areas that should be thinned particularly heavily to encourage the devel-

**Table 10.1   Forestry operations in Belvoir Park Forest for the period 1991/92–1995/96**

|  | 1991/92 | 1992/93 | 1993/94 | 1994/95 | 1995/96 |
|---|---|---|---|---|---|
| Planting (ha) | - | 1 | 2 | - | - |
| Weeding (ha) | 3 | 2 | 2 | - | - |
| Drains maintenance (ha) | 4 | 2 | 7 | 10 | 6 |
| Cleaning (ha) | 10 | 8 | 7 | - | 3 |
| Thinning (m$^3$) | - | 200 | 410 | 300 | - |
| Felling (m$^3$) | 380 | - | - | - | - |

opment of a desirable and attractive woodland structure. All forestry operations are subject to the recreation and landscape development plan and will be modified as necessary to satisfy this objective.

# For more information

## Advice

Department of Agriculture for Northern Ireland, Forest Service, Dundonald House, Upper Newtownards Road, Belfast, BT4 3SB.

# Index

Printed in the United Kingdom for HMSO
Dd 297423 C50 5/95 552 12521